MONEY
for ADULTING
Fun Tips and Financial Tricks FOR TEENS

Michelle Hung, CFA

ILLUSTRATIONS BY DREW BARDANA

callisto
publishing
an imprint of Sourcebooks

Art Director: Richard Tapp and Lisa Schreiber
Art Producer: Hannah Dickerson
Editor: Barbara J. Isenberg
Production Manager: Riley Hoffman
Production Editor: Melissa Edeburn
Graphic Designer: Erin Rinker

Published by Callisto Publishing LLC C/O Sourcebooks LLC
P.O. Box 4410, Naperville, Illinois 60567-4410
(630) 961-3900
callistopublishing.com

Originally published as *Investing for Teens* in 2022 in the United States of
America by Callisto Teens, an imprint of Callisto Publishing LLC. This edition
issued based on the paperback edition published in 2022 in the United
States of America by Callisto Teens, an imprint of Callisto Publishing LLC.

Library of Congress Cataloging-in-Publication Data is on file with
the publisher.

Printed and bound in China.
OGP 10 9 8 7 6 5 4 3 2 1

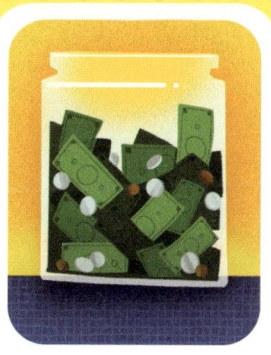

To my family and best friends.
Thank you for your continued
support and love.

CONTENTS

How to Use This Book **viii**

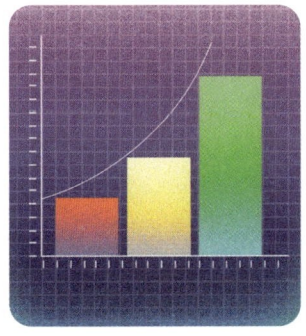

HOW TO USE THIS BOOK

What if I told you that many millionaires in America are (and I bet this wouldn't even cross your mind) . . . TEACHERS!

That's right! Imagine how many teachers you have met and will meet in your lifetime. Chances are, some of them are millionaires. Millionaires are not just CEOs of billion-dollar companies or entrepreneurs that developed an app and sold it for a gazillion dollars to a tech giant.

This book isn't about how to become a millionaire. It's a money and **investing** guide to starting your own wealth-building journey. It will help you make excellent financial decisions that can give you a head start in life. A head start is one of the greatest advantages you'll have over any adult out there—including CEOs. How so, you wonder?

Let me introduce you to Susie. When Susie was thirteen years old, she started getting a consistent flow of money from a $10 weekly allowance. She took on part-time jobs and eventually attended college. Susie was really great at saving money until college. That's when she got her first **credit** card. More on what those are later. From that point on, Susie made poor money decisions that led her to a mountain of **debt** by the time she graduated.

This person was me. I was a Susie Spender. I bought so many things I couldn't afford simply because I thought

I was being an adult. At that time, I thought adulting meant being able to do whatever I wanted—including buying whatever I wanted! This attitude put me into debt. Eventually I was able to pay off my debt, build my savings, and grow my money by investing it in the **stock markets**. By the time I was thirty years old, I had built up over $120,000 in my investment **portfolio**.

Then life hit me with several difficult situations. My twelve-year relationship ended, I lost my full-time job of seven years, and my dog passed away—all around the same time. But this time around, I was able to navigate life's circumstances a bit better because I did not have to worry about money.

Thanks to those harsh lessons in my twenties, difficult life events in my thirties, and my education and work experience in finance, I now help thousands of people across North America get out of debt, save money, and grow their wealth through investing.

In the following pages, I will show you ways to earn money and save it. I will also show you what to do with that saved money so you can start growing your wealth (and not end up being a Susie Spender). Although your money journey will be unique and personal, this book is structured in a way that is easy to follow. There are also lots of step-by-step guided exercises you can do on your own and with the help of your guardian.

Happy investing!

Making Money

B efore you can start investing money, you're going to need some! But first, let's dive into understanding what money is, where it came from, why we have money, and how it's created today.

Have you ever wondered how small pieces of paper and metal discs became the things people use to buy *everything*? And how many of us around the world came to agree that they would be the primary forms of payment people should use and accept in exchange for goods and services? In this chapter, we're going to go through a brief history of what money is, how it has evolved over time, and how to earn money for yourself by getting a job or starting your own business.

A Brief History of Money

Before the creation of paper money or **currency** (regulated coins were first used in 600 BCE), people simply traded products and services. Daniella was good at making boots. Patrick was a skilled fisherman. If Patrick needed boots, he would trade fish he caught for boots Daniella made. This method was the bartering system.

Bartering became more difficult as the population grew and foreigners from other countries wanted to trade. The solution was to standardize an object that could be used to freely trade goods. Currency was born. Things like cowrie shells, corn, and even whale teeth were used as currency at different points in time.

Eventually gold became a standard currency and was widespread across the globe. Kings and rulers mined gold and silver, turned them into coins, stamped them for authenticity, and declared them *the* currency to be used. Once a ruler deemed something to be *the* currency, everyone obliged. It's how value is created. When a collective group deems something valuable, it *is*.

Over time, paper money replaced gold coins, which is how the "gold standard" was developed. Instead of circulating gold coins for people to use, paper money was issued in the form of a promissory note. The note stated that anyone could exchange it at any time for gold bullion (99% pure gold)—at a fixed price. Of course, the government fixed the prices!

Today no country uses the gold standard. Instead, **fiat currency** is the primary currency. It is government-issued money that is not backed by a physical commodity or good. Because fiat currency is not backed by anything, like gold, an unlimited supply can circulate in an economy.

Mint Condition

Remember how I said kings and rulers would just mint gold coins, stamp them for authenticity, and then declare them as *the* currency to be used? Not much has changed over several millennia. The United States Mint, which is more than two hundred years old, creates and manufactures coins like pennies, dimes, nickels, and quarters. The U.S. Mint's job is to ensure there are coins available for people to spend, collect, and save. Each year, the U.S. Mint creates ten billion circulating coins! The Mint does not print paper money. That's the job of the Bureau of Engraving and Printing.

The U.S. Mint has another job. It stores and protects the country's gold. Even though the gold standard is no longer used, the government still holds on to gold reserves. About half of the country's gold is stored in Fort Knox, Kentucky, at the United States Bullion Depository.

The Mint also produces collectible memorabilia coins, coins for investment purposes (they are usually pure gold or silver), and award medals that honor people and institutions for their distinguished achievements in making the country or world a better place. These medals are the Congressional Gold Medals for Congress and they are the highest expression of appreciation issued by Congress. Maybe one day you'll receive one!

MONEY MATTERS: CURRENCY

Here is a brief timeline of how currency has evolved:

9000–6000 BCE: Cattle (and other livestock) becomes the first form of money.

1200 BCE: Cowrie shells are first used in China and are the most widely and longest-used currency in history.

1000 BCE: Bronze and copper cowrie-shaped coins are made in China.

600 BCE: Regulated coins are used for the first time in the Lydian Empire.

118 BCE: Leather money is used in China and could be considered the first documented banknotes.

806: Paper banknotes become widely used in China from the ninth to the fifteenth century.

1535: Wampum (beads created from clam or whelk shells) are used by Indigenous people in North America as currency.

1816: The gold standard is created.

1930: Fiat currency takes over as the world's primary currency.

2009: Cryptocurrency, a new form of digital currency, is created by people (not the government!) using computer code, making it difficult to counterfeit.

Earning Your Own Money

Let's get down to how you can earn some moolah on your own. Perhaps you've received money from adults, or maybe you are working a part-time job already! If you don't have a part-time job, or you hate the one you have now, let's explore some options.

GETTING A PART-TIME JOB

Many places hire teens on a part-time basis, making it possible to work after school and on weekends. Check your local grocery stores, coffee shops, or any other retailers in your neighborhood. Ask someone at the store if they're hiring. If they are, find out if there's an application form you need to complete. Ask an adult to help you fill out the form.

Depending on the state you live in, a minor (anyone under eighteen years old) may be required to provide a **work permit** or **certificate of age**. Check with your school guidance office to see if they can provide the forms needed or if they can direct you somewhere else to get the form. You may also be asked for a reference letter written by someone who can vouch for you. Ask a teacher, a coach, or another trusted adult who knows you well for a reference letter.

Before pursuing a part-time job, consider how having that job will impact the other areas of your life. Will it interfere with any after-school activities—like sports or babysitting a younger sibling? How will you get to the job? Can you walk, bike, or drive yourself, or will someone need to take you? How many hours can you commit to it per week? Does the job require you to work late?

Make sure you ask the employer what kind of hours are required for the job before you commit, and get permission from your guardian before you take a part-time job!

GET A SUMMER JOB

If you're a busy bee during the school year, then perhaps a summer job would be more ideal. Many places hire students during the summer break, like summer camps, farmers' markets, farms, amusement parks, swimming pools, or companies that hire summer interns for their offices. I was a camp counselor for three summers in a row and it was a great experience (also exhausting!).

A huge benefit of a summer job is the opportunity to focus on working full-time and saving money, so you don't have to work during the school year. We'll discuss savings in the next chapter.

START YOUR OWN BUSINESS

What if you can't commit to a regular schedule that a part-time or summer job requires, and you want to set your own hours? You can create your own schedule by starting your own business! You can provide a service such as babysitting, mowing lawns, shoveling snow, walking dogs, or tutoring. Another option is to create something and sell it in person or online. Things like jewelry, baked goods, or other crafts are great ideas. Be creative!

You can't expect business to pour in if nobody knows what you're selling. You must market yourself. Share your business on social media; post a flyer at your local community center, café, or library (get permission first); tell your friends and neighbors; and post to online marketplaces. Any time you post to an online marketplace, be sure to get permission and guidance from an adult in your household. People pay hourly for services like babysitting, dog walking, or tutoring. Do some research online and see what others are charging for the same service or product in your area before coming up with your fee.

When it comes to your products, you want to ensure you cover your costs *and* make a profit. For example, let's say you want to sell candles, and the cost of ingredients and tools is $50. If you make 36 candles, your cost per candle will be: $50/36 = $1.39.

If you charge $1.39 per candle, you'll break even (get back what you invested). But you don't want that—you want to make a profit! If you double the price of each candle, you'll get $2.78 each. Let's round up to $3.00 per candle. Your profit will be the price you charge, minus your cost, multiplied by the number of candles you make: ($3.00 – $1.39) × 36 = $57.96 profit.

If it took you four hours to prep, make, and sell everything, you'd be making: $57.96/4 = $14.49 per hour. Not bad!

WHAT BENEFITS AND RESULTS DOES YOUR BUSINESS PROVIDE?

A business is all about providing a solution to a problem people have. Every business sells a solution. When you provide a dog-walking service, you are helping someone free up their time. When you tutor, you are helping someone improve on a subject they are struggling with. When you sell cupcakes, you are satisfying someone's sweet tooth. Think of the results and benefits your service or product provides and make a list of them. For example, if you'd like to tutor someone in math, you would might write something like this:

Benefits of hiring a tutor:

⇨ Child receives help in a one-on-one setting.

⇨ Parents/guardians can enjoy extra free time.

⇨ Child is less frustrated.

Results of hiring a tutor:

⇨ Child gets better grades.

⇨ Child becomes more confident in math.

⇨ Child enjoys math more.

You can use these lists when you market your services on flyers or online. Be careful not to overpromise, underdeliver, or exaggerate results!

SELL YOUR OLD STUFF

Selling stuff is a great way to clear out things you don't need in your home while making money in the process. Go through your closets, basement, and attic, and ask everyone in your house for stuff they don't need. Then sell it! Be sure to get permission from the adults in your household before you do so.

You can sell things several ways:

→ Host a yard or garage sale and post some flyers in your neighborhood to let people know when it's happening.

→ List items on an online marketplace (get permission from an adult).

→ Share items on social media.

If you want to sell something online, snap a few photos for people to see (make it look appealing!).

You might know that Rihanna has sold more than sixty million albums and won eight Grammy Awards. But did you know she is a billionaire thanks, in part, to her businesses in the fashion and beauty industry?

Rihanna signed her first music contract when she was seventeen years old. Within three years, she won her first Grammy Award. By the time she was twenty-nine, Rihanna branched out of music and acting and tapped into other creative outlets. She launched inclusive makeup and lingerie businesses that serve the needs of Black women and women of all body types.

Rihanna is a great example of how you can find multiple ways to earn money outside your primary talent. Today she is the wealthiest female musician in the world and a global fashion icon.

Check Your Pay

When you start working, be aware that not all the money you earn will go into your pocket! You will pay a variety of taxes on your income. The **Internal Revenue Service (IRS)** will take a cut of your paycheck, whether you're working part-time at a store or running your own business. When you receive your pay stub from your part-time job, you'll see that employment taxes have been deducted automatically. They cover federal and state taxes, social security, and Medicare.

When you are self-employed and have made more than $400, you'll have to file a tax return and pay taxes on the profits of your business. Your taxable income is the amount that's taxed *after* your expenses have been deducted. Let's say you sold bracelets online last year and you made $2,000 in sales. If the cost of your materials, packaging, shipping, online listing fees, and labor (yes, pay yourself a wage!) amounted to $1,200, your taxable income is: $2,000 – $1,200 = $800.

The self-employment tax rate fluctuates, so be sure to check how much it is before you calculate how much you need to set aside to pay it. For example, if the rate is 15.3%, you would need to set aside $122.40 for the IRS: $800 × 0.153 = $122.40. So before you start your own business, consider all the costs of running and starting the business—and the taxes you'll owe the IRS (and set that money aside!).

EXPERT TIP

Sales is an important life skill, and it's not just for business owners or sales roles. When you apply for jobs, you will usually go through an interview process. That's where you must sell (or market) yourself so they hire you over others. I highly recommend you read books, review blogs, or watch online videos on how to sell yourself.

CREATE A LIST OF WAYS TO EARN MONEY

Try coming up with a list of ways to earn money and what you'll need to do to make them happen. You don't have to choose one method over another when it comes to earning money. You can do more than one thing if you are able to balance them with everything else in your life. For example, you can have a full-time summer job, but also sell digital art online throughout the year.

When choosing where to apply for a job, consider some of the perks that come with it, like discounts. Maybe your friends already work at a particular store, so you'd enjoy the atmosphere. When brainstorming possible places to work, think about your interests, what you're good at, and how you can help people. You are investing your time, so you want to make sure you're happy doing your job and not stressing yourself out!

Keeping Your Money Safe

You've earned money—now what? Be a Susie Spender like I was? Of course not!

In ninth grade, I received an allowance ($10) at the beginning of every week and had to make sure the money lasted Monday through Saturday. I stored any leftover money in a pouch I hid in my closet. Over time, that money accumulated until I had a pile of cash sitting in my closet. I felt so rich! It wasn't until I had my wallet stolen at school (with cash in it) that I decided it was time to open a bank account and keep a **debit card** on hand instead of a wad of cash.

Putting your cash in a bank account, rather than keeping it at home or in a wallet, is the safest way to store your money because:

1. Cash can be lost or stolen.

2. Cash can be destroyed, like in a fire.

A bank account also offers benefits, such as:

1. **Convenience:** When you open a bank account, the bank will issue you a debit card that allows you to pay for things from your account at stores or online. You can even take cash out of an ATM.

2. **More money:** That's right, your money can earn money for you in the form of **interest**. Believe it or not, the bank will pay you to store your money there!

3. **Protection from theft:** Unless a thief knows your debit card's PIN (secret code), it will be very difficult to steal money from your bank account.

This brings us to your next probable question . . .

Is my money safe at the bank?

The federal government created an agency called the Federal Deposit Insurance Corporation (FDIC) to protect people's money while it is stored at various financial institutions, like banks, **credit unions**, and **brokerages**. Money you keep in these institutions is insured (protected) from theft, fraud, and even the institution itself—in case they go out of business, for example. Because of these protective measures, you can be sure your money is safe at the bank.

When you open a bank account, you can choose from several options:

Bank: Banks are for-profit institutions that offer a wide range of financial products, such as loans, credit cards, and **mortgages**.

Credit Union: Credit unions are similar to banks, except they are nonprofit institutions created through a cooperative—a group of members that share a common bond, such as the industry they work in, their religious interest, or the community they live in.

Brokerage: If you want to invest your money in the stock market, you'll need this type of account to store your **stock** investments (more on this later).

How do you choose which type of bank account to go with? We'll discuss banking in more detail in the next chapter.

Check Your Bottom Line

What you've learned in this chapter:

⮥ How the system of money was created

⮥ The evolution of currency

⮥ Ways to earn money: through a job, selling stuff, or starting your own business

⮥ What deductions are taken from your pay, such as taxes

⮥ How to keep your money safe

CHAPTER 2

Saving Money

I've spent many years observing people's finances—their income, spending, and saving. The biggest difference between people who are savers and those who are in debt is *how much they spend*. I've seen people drowning in debt who make extremely high incomes ($100,000+ per year)—and others earning *half* that amount with large savings accounts.

This chapter is important because a lot of people's day-to-day stresses are related to money. They are either not saving enough money or deeply in debt. In this chapter, I am going to show you how to save money, explain what financial goals are and how you can set yours, talk about what a **budget** is and how to create one, show you how to grow your money while it is at the bank, and, of course, alert you to the dangers of debt. You'll see that the amount of money you make is less important than how you spend and save it.

Spending vs. Saving

When I received my first paycheck at my first job, I was so excited! Back then, I was making $6.85 per hour. I worked ten to fifteen hours a week and got paid biweekly (every two weeks), so my paychecks were somewhere between $120 and $180.

I thought about all the clothes I could buy and how I'd be able to buy whatever else I wanted, whenever I wanted. That wasn't really the case, but I felt that way at first! I quickly stopped myself when I realized how hard I had worked for that money. I spent hours standing on my feet as a cashier dealing with grumpy customers. Did I do it just so I could blow my paycheck on clothes? No thanks!

I was very careful with my money. I kept track of how much I spent and made sure I wasn't spending more than what I earned in one paycheck. My biggest fear was looking at my savings account one day and having a zero balance! If I blew all my money on things I didn't need, I wouldn't have anything left for things I did need—like food! This possibility is why it's important to save money.

At some point, you'll be responsible for paying your own bills—like rent, electricity, internet, cell phone, taxes, etc. If you ever lose your job or are unable to work, you'll need to be able to pay for those things without relying on a paycheck. You'll have to use your savings. This is called saving for an emergency.

Another reason to save money is for major purchases. Do you have your eye on an expensive item, like a laptop or a trip abroad after graduation? These purchases require some time to save.

Here's an example:

You want to buy a laptop that costs $1,500. At your job, you make $300 every two weeks, after taxes. This means you make $600 per month. Let's say, between buying lunches and going out with your friends, you spend $60 each week—$240 per month. This leaves you with $600 − $240 = $360 per month in savings.

If you saved $360 every month, you would be able to buy that laptop in just over four months ($1,500/$360 = 4.167 months)! What if you wanted the laptop in three months? You'll need to be more aggressive with your savings. It would mean spending less money during the week, or even working a few extra hours at your job.

When I was in twelfth grade, my school soccer team took a trip to Hawaii for a tournament. Many of my teammates, myself included, worked extra hours and saved for a long time (we had more than a year and half's notice). We ended up being one of the worst teams at the tournament and lost every game, but It was a memorable and enjoyable experience nonetheless. I ended up spending all my savings on that one trip, but it was worth it! Looking back, I should have set aside at least $100 so I didn't come home to zero dollars in my bank account!

Setting Goals

It's important to set financial goals not only because they give you a reason to save money (as opposed to blowing it all) but also because many personal goals are tied to a financial goal. For example, if you want to become a better singer, you might want to hire a vocal coach, which requires money. Over time, your financial goals will become more expensive, like saving for your college education or buying a house.

The higher the price tag, the longer it will take to save for the goal. Any goal that takes five years or more to reach is considered a long-term financial goal. Medium-term goals are those in the three- to five-year range. For example, if you're in tenth grade and are planning to go to college or technical school right after graduation, saving for that additional education is a medium-term goal. Goals that take three years or less to reach are called short-term goals. My trip to Hawaii was a short-term financial goal because I had one and a half years to save.

It's important to recognize how long your financial goals will take so you can decide whether to save or invest your money. You save money for short-term goals. You invest money for long-term goals. It's also important to be able to balance your daily spending while reaching your financial goals—even multiple ones at once. That's where a budget comes in. Read on to find out how.

WHAT ARE YOUR GOALS?

Let's plan out your financial goals!

	Short-Term Goal (less than 3 years)	Medium-Term Goal (3 to 5 years)	Long-Term Goal (5+ years)
How much will you need for this goal?			
What is your deadline for achieving this goal?			
How much time do you have to save for your goal?			
How much will you need to save each month to reach your goal?			

Here's an example of how to work out a short-term goal:

GOAL: OUT-OF-CITY SOCCER TOURNAMENT

Amount I need for goal: $600

When I need the money: September 30, 2025

Time to save: 6 months

Savings timeline: $100 per month for 6 months

Did you know that plenty of celebrities, athletes, and even billionaires are super careful with their money and keep themselves on a budget? Ed Sheeran revealed in an interview that he gives himself an allowance of $1,000 per month. He apparently spends most of it on taxis! He invests most of the money he earns and admitted that if he left all the money in his account, he'd just spend it all!

Investor Warren Buffett, one of the top ten richest people on the planet, still lives in the same house he bought in 1958 for $31,500! He is known to live a very frugal life. He eats at fast-food places like McDonald's, uses coupons, and wears non-designer clothes—despite being a billionaire! Both people invest their wealth and find ways to make themselves even richer.

Creating a Budget

A budget is a system that helps you organize your expenses relative to your income. Budgets are important. They help you save money, reach your financial goals, and ensure you don't overspend—or worse, end up in debt!

Following are three popular ways to budget. Choose one or try all three to see which works best for you.

THE 50/30/20 BUDGET RULE

This system is easiest because it allocates, or places, your after-tax income into three generic categories:

1. 50% toward needs

2. 30% toward wants (fun spending)

3. 20% toward savings and goals

For example, if you earn $800 per month from your part-time job, your budget may look like this:

INCOME: $800

50% NEEDS: $400
30% WANTS: $240
20% SAVINGS: $160

The 50/30/20 rule is simply a general rule on how to allocate your income. It may not work if you have more aggressive goals and want to save more than 20%. In that case, the next method may work better.

ZERO-BUDGETING

This method takes the previous system a step further by allocating your income into specific categories. It's called zero-budgeting because it allocates *all* your income, while making sure your income is equal to your expenses. It's great if you want to track your expenses very closely.

It may look something like this:

PAY YOURSELF FIRST

This method is my favorite, and it's very effective with my students and clients. It prioritizes savings and goals. Often people spend money on everything else before even thinking about saving money. This method guarantees money goes into savings each month.

First, divide your expenses into two categories: **fixed expenses** and **variable expenses**. Fixed expenses are predictable in price and recurrence, like your cell phone, monthly bus pass, and TV streaming services. You know when to pay these and how much. Your savings and goals are fixed expenses. Variable expenses are less predictable and will vary monthly and weekly. They are things like groceries, eating out, and movie tickets, which fluctuate based on how you feel like spending.

Next, allocate money toward your fixed expenses—including your savings and goals. Then take the money that's left and divide it by the number of weeks in the month (usually four). Treat that balance like an allowance and spend it any way you want.

It will look something like this:

INCOME: $800

FIXED EXPENSES & SAVINGS: $440
Rent to parents: $200
Cell phone: $60
Trip: $120
Savings: $60

VARIABLE EXPENSES: $360
Weekly allowance: $360/4 = $90

Be sure to revise your budget regularly to make sure you're on track with your spending and savings, especially if your income varies each month.

QUIZ TIME!

1. With a 50/30/20 budget, how is your money divided?
   a) **50% needs, 30% wants, 20% savings**

   b) **50% wants, 30% savings, 20% needs**

   c) **50% savings, 30% needs, 20% wants**

2. If you want to keep a close eye on all your spending, which budgeting method is the best?
   a) **50/30/20 budget**

   b) **Zero-budgeting**

   c) **Pay yourself first**

3. Variable expenses are:
   a) **Predictable in price**

   b) **Recurring**

   c) **Unpredictable and subject to change**

4. Fixed expenses are:
   a) **Predictable in price and recurrence**

   b) **Unpredictable**

   c) **Very high**

5. If you're afraid you might spend everything before you save, the best budgeting method for you would be:

a) **50/30/20 budget**

b) **Zero-budgeting**

c) **Pay yourself first**

6. Budgets are important because:

a) **They help you save money for goals.**

b) **They help keep you out of debt.**

c) **Both of the above.**

ANSWERS: (1) a; (2) b; (3) c; (4) a; (5) c; (6) c

Take It to the Bank

In chapter 1 (page 1), we discussed the various institutions you can use to store your money: banks, credit unions, and brokerages. Banks were created because people needed a safe place to store their gold where they could retrieve it easily. Bankers eventually realized that most people didn't retrieve their money often. They started lending out the money and charged a fee, called interest, to the people borrowing it. Customers who keep money at the bank receive some of that interest.

There are two main accounts you can open at a bank: a checking account and a savings account.

Checking Account: This account is best used for everyday activities, such as withdrawals, paying bills online, and making purchases through a linked debit card. Money moves in and out frequently, so you will be paid very little interest, if any, on this account.

Savings Account: This account is made for long-term money storage. You can leave your money here and earn some interest. It won't be a lot, but it's better than nothing!

When people are not depositing money at banks, they are borrowing from them. Banks provide a variety of loans and credit services to their customers so purchases are more accessible to them. A very common loan is a credit card. Instead of paying cash or using money directly from your savings account, a credit card allows you to make purchases before actually paying for them. They make people's purchasing experience easier.

Your credit is based on your ability to repay what you've borrowed. If you pay back the full borrowed amount on time—which is usually within thirty days of making the purchase—you don't have to pay any interest on it, which is great! If you don't repay the full amount, you end up in borrowing territory. This means you must pay the bank interest for lending you money. That interest penalty doesn't end until you pay the full amount back.

The interest rates on credit cards are usually very high (around 20% per year!), and the banks tell you this information upfront when they first issue the card. Paying on time and repaying the full amount shows the bank you're a trustworthy (creditworthy) borrower. In the future, when you need to borrow money for bigger purchases (like a house), they can give you more favorable terms, like a lower interest rate.

Some accounts require a monthly maintenance fee, but it can usually be waived for students. Having both a savings and checking account is ideal so you can separate the money you save from the money you spend. If you are under eighteen years old, you'll need an adult with you to open any of these accounts.

MONEY MATTERS: BEWARE OF CREDIT CARD DEBT

Debt allows people to purchase items they can't pay for right away. Debts for things like a house, college, or business loan are good because they have an **asset** attached to them. That means there is a future benefit or **return**. When debt is used for things that don't provide a future return, particularly purchases made on a credit card, it can be dangerous. The scary thing about credit cards and loans is they give people the illusion of having a lot of spending power. Always remember that your credit limit is not your monthly budget!

I was introduced to my first credit card when I was on my university campus. Credit card companies often offer people goodies, such as free gym bags, so they sign up—and hopefully rack up a lot of debt! I was given a $5,000 credit card limit when I was twenty years old. I ended up owing a ton by the time I graduated. It was NOT a good way to start life after school!

Taking Interest

One of the biggest benefits of leaving your money at a bank is earning money through interest payments. The bank will pay you an amount, quoted as an **annual**

percentage yield (APY), for keeping your money with them. The APY determines how much you will earn at the end of one year.

For example, if you leave $1,000 in your savings account and the bank pays you an APY of 0.5%, in one year, you'll have $1,005. How much will you have after twenty years? Let's go through the two main types of interest and their calculations.

SIMPLE INTEREST

Let's assume the bank pays you an annual interest rate of 3%. Note: 3% is high for a savings account and it's unlikely you'll receive that much, but we'll use it just for illustration purposes. **Principal** is equal to the original amount of your deposit, and "n" is the number of periods—in this case, years.

The formula to calculate how much your savings will be worth using simple interest is:

Principal × (1 + interest rate × n) = Savings total

If you deposit $1,000 (the principal) and earn 3% per year, after one year your money will be worth:

$1,000 × [1 + (0.03 x 20)] = $1,030

After 20 years, your money will be worth:

$1,000 × [1 + (0.03 x 20)]

$1,000 × (1.6) = $1,600

You earn $600 in total interest payments over 20 years.

Here is what your money growth will look like:

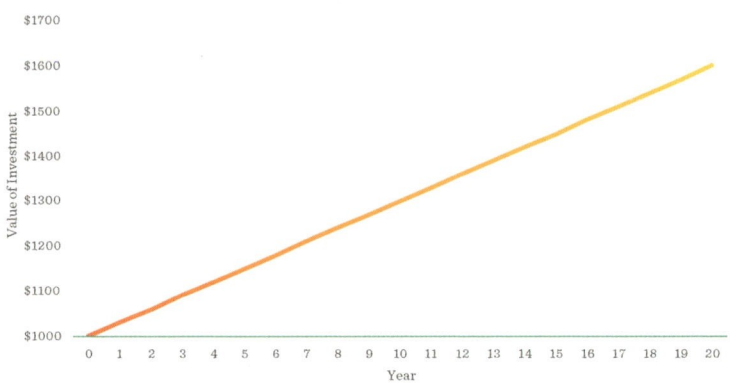

Value of $1,000 over 20 Years with Simple Interest

When you earn interest in a savings account, you're probably not going to remove that money from your account—at least I hope you don't! But that's what simple interest is based on—*not* reinvesting what you earn. Ideally, you want to leave the earned interest in the account and earn interest on top of that interest. It's called **compound interest**, and we'll get to it in the next section.

Simple interest is usually calculated on loans like **personal loans**, **lines of credit**, and mortgages, where interest is only calculated on the initial principal amount. You'll want to pay the least amount of interest on loans, which means avoiding loans with compound interest—like credit cards!

COMPOUND INTEREST

You'll want the money you are saving to compound. In other words, you want to earn money on top of the money you've already earned. But when you're paying interest, you definitely don't want it to compound. This type of interest is why it takes people a long time to pay off credit cards when they are just making the minimum payment!

Again, principal is equal to the original amount of your deposit, and "n" is the number of periods—in this case, years. The formula to calculate the value of your money when using compound interest is:

Principal × (1 + interest rate)^n = Value of money

There is no need to do these calculations by hand! A simple search online for "compound interest calculator" will give you the tools to figure it out.

Here is how much $1,000 would be worth if you *re-invest* all the interest payments you receive (and leave all the earned money in the account) for twenty years, and are paid 3% per year:

$1,000 × (1 + 0.03)^{20} = $1,806.11

That's $806.11 in earned interest after twenty years, compared with $600 with simple interest had you *not* reinvested the interest you earned.

That's a difference of $806.11 – $600 = $206.11

You might think it doesn't seem like a whole lot, but when you start investing money and earning a higher return, the difference will be massive.

Here is what your money growth would look like:

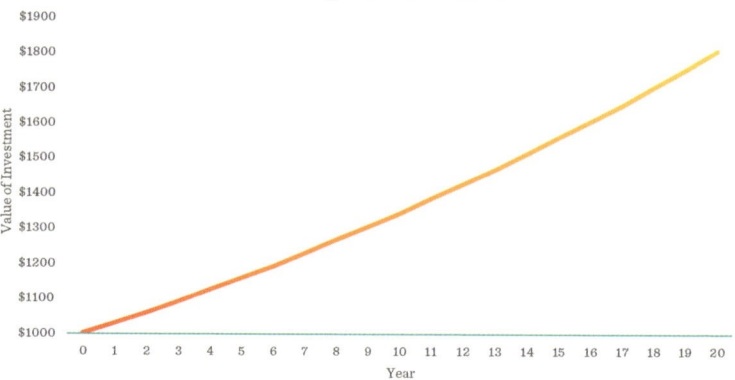

Value of $1,000 over Twenty Years with Compound Interest

EXPERT TIP

Set up automatic deposits that put money into your savings account each time you get paid. For example, if you get paid on the tenth and twenty-fifth every month, and you plan on saving $100 each month, set up pre-authorized automatic deposits of $50 into your savings account on the eleventh and twenty-six of each month.

Check Your Bottom Line

What you've learned in this chapter:

⇨ The importance of saving money

⇨ How to create a budget using three methods

⇨ How to set financial goals

⇨ The types of accounts you can open at a bank or credit union

⇨ The dangers of debt and what good debt is

⇨ The difference between simple interest and compound interest

CHAPTER 3

Investing 101

When we discussed financial goals in chapter 2, I mentioned that it is important to categorize your goals by timeline because money set aside for long-term goals should be treated differently than money for short-term goals. Money for long-term goals will be invested, and that's the focus of this chapter. You'll learn what investing is, why it's important, and how to do it.

Investing is using money in a way that provides a future return for you. You can invest in things like property, businesses, art, or anything else that grows in value over time. This chapter focuses on investing in companies. I describe investing in companies like this: You are investing in your day-to-day life.

Everything you buy, from the food you eat at restaurants, to the clothes you wear, to the phones you use, comes from companies that make money every time you spend money. You can invest in a company by buying their stock, thus becoming a small owner of that company. Being an owner means you are entitled to some of the profits they make.

Why Invest?

Take a guess at who the richest people are. Entrepreneurs, CEOs, and investors are some of the richest people in the world. What do they all have in common? Ownership in assets, like real estate or businesses. Some of these people own and work in one business directly, whereas others just own multiple businesses. When you own an asset, like a business, there's no limit to how successful it can become. The profits can be unlimited. Imagine being able to get your hands on them!

Not only can you make a lot of money by investing, it is also one of the easiest ways to make money. Your money grows while you sleep, go to school, and work. There's no need to hustle or sell anything to anybody. It is called **passive income**. Your money grows while you live your life. Imagine having more than one source of income—you have your job, and you have your investments working for you. Amazing, right? The longer you allow your money to grow, and the earlier you start investing, the less money you'll need to save to reach those long-term goals.

Remember we discussed compound interest in a savings account (page 33)? It works the same way with investing! You reinvest the profits that are paid to you from your investments. Then *that* money will earn money as well. Time is your best friend when investing, so the younger you start, the better off you'll be financially. You can start right now—even with $10 or $20 per month. You'll just need an adult to assist you with the investing process.

One year, I took a trip to Hawaii (as an adult) and met a woman named Sam. She was twenty-four years old and had just moved to Hawaii because she wanted to surf every day! When I told her I teach people how to invest for a living, she told me her investing story. Sam received an allowance from her parents as a child and was required to invest a portion of it. Sam's dad asked her what companies she liked, and he invested her money into those companies.

By the time she was twenty-four, Sam's investments had grown to $25,000! As a result, she felt financially secure enough to quit her full-time job in Colorado and move to Hawaii to start a new life. Sam is ever so thankful that her parents helped her invest from a very young age.

Risk vs. Reward

There's a saying in the finance world: "There's no such thing as a free lunch." No, this isn't about food! It means there's always a cost to something you want to do. In the investing world, the cost is risk—the risk of losing your money. There's no reward if you take no risk, and the more risk you take, the higher the potential reward. This is what is meant when we say there are no free lunches. You can't get something—whether that's a free lunch or a high reward—for nothing.

If you come across something or someone promising you extremely high returns with very little risk, it is likely a scam. Be aware of this type of scheme because when it comes to money, there are a lot of scam artists out there. People have lost life savings after being duped. If it's too good to be true, it probably is.

Okay, so why would anyone take any risk if the risk is losing their money? Why would you want to lose money? There are two reasons:

1. There are ways to manage risk so you don't lose all your money (we'll discuss them later).
2. If you don't take risks, you won't make any money!

LOW RISK

I once came across a blog about a girl—let's call her Jane—who documented her investment journey. When Jane was sixteen, she went to the bank with her mom to invest her savings. When the bank teller asked her, "How much risk do you want to take with your money?" Jane instinctively answered, "No risk. I don't want to lose any money."

Years passed and as Jane looked at her investments, she couldn't understand why her money didn't really grow. After doing her own research, she realized she was invested in very low-risk products called **bonds**. Because of the bonds' low risk, Jane had barely made any money over ten years.

Of course, Jane was very disappointed. Not only did she have tiny returns on her money, but she had also thought she was doing her future self a favor by investing. She didn't really hurt herself, though, because technically she didn't lose money. The problem was she didn't make as much money as she thought and lost ten years of investing time. The positive thing was she was still very young when she realized it and had many decades of investing ahead of her.

Bonds are an example of something that is low risk. You won't make much money, but you won't lose much money, either.

HIGH RISK

Remember the richest people in the world I talked about earlier? Those investors became successful by taking risk. Entrepreneurs invest their time, effort, and probably life savings into their businesses—and they own stock in their own businesses.

Some businesses work out, and some don't. Investing in stocks is considered high risk (higher than bonds) because if a business doesn't work out, it can go bankrupt, and people who invested in those businesses lose their money. If the business is successful, however, the profits are unlimited! Higher risk means higher returns.

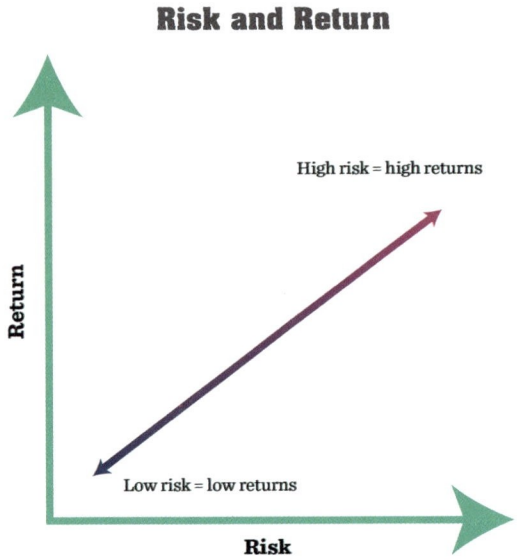

Risk and Return

High risk = high returns

Return

Low risk = low returns

Risk

RISK TOLERANCE

In all my years of looking at people's investment port-folios, I've found that one of the biggest mistakes people make is not taking enough risk. There are A LOT of Janes out there—people who unknowingly express their disdain for risk and then end up in low-risk invest-ments that earn them very little. Not taking enough risk is a risk in itself. People miss out on returns simply because of their misunderstanding of risk. But how much risk *should* you take?

One of the main factors that determines your risk tolerance is your age. The earlier in life you invest, and the longer the timeline you give your investments to grow, the more risk you can take. That's because if something goes wrong with your investments, like their value decreases temporarily, you have time to recover.

When you're investing in companies, it takes time for those companies to grow. When they release new products or expand their projects, they can generate more profits, but it takes time. Investors may not see money gains for a long time, which is why you should invest only the money set aside for long-term goals.

In the short term, stock prices can decrease. If you need quick access to cash, the last thing you'd want to do is sell your stocks at a loss. So another question to ask yourself is "Can I afford to lose this money?" If your answer is no because you need to access the cash soon or you just don't feel good about it, your risk tolerance will be lower. The last thing you want is to lose sleep over your money!

LIQUIDITY

The money in your savings account is available for you to withdraw any time you need it. This availability is called liquidity, which is a measure of how easy it is to turn an investment into cash. Cash is the most liquid asset—because it's already cash!

When you determine the liquidity of an investment, think about how quickly it can be converted into cash. The longer and more difficult it is, the less liquid it is. Housing and real estate, for example, are not liquid. If you were selling a house, you'd have to list it for sale, find a buyer that will make an offer, etc. It can be a very lengthy process, and you may not see the cash from the sale of your home for months!

Your need to access cash quickly will also determine your risk tolerance and your investments.

WHAT'S YOUR RISK TOLERANCE?

Let's determine your tolerance for risk by answering some questions:

1. Would you feel okay if the potential for your invest-ment to grow from $500 to $900 comes with the potential of seeing your investment shrink from $500 to $300?

   a) **Yes**

   b) **No**

2. If you invest in high-risk stuff, like stocks, are you prepared to lose it all if the investment doesn't work out?

   a) **Yes**

   b) **No**

3. Are you okay with not touching your investments for a long time (five-plus years)?

   a) **Yes**

   b) **No**

4. Are the goals you want to achieve more than five years away?

   a) Yes

   b) No

If you answered yes three or more times, you have a high risk tolerance.

If you answered yes twice and no twice, you have a medium risk tolerance.

If you answered no three or more times, you have a low risk tolerance.

MONEY MATTERS: SAVING FOR COLLEGE

One of the biggest financial decisions (and investments) you'll make is your college education. Depending on where you attend college, the cost of tuition (classes) varies. Tuition isn't the only college cost, though. Other college expenses to factor in are:

◇ Cost of books

◇ Cost of living expenses, like room/rent, food

◇ Cost of interest on loans, as you'll likely be borrowing money

When you add everything up, the cost of college is massive. The average cost of tuition in the United States is $35,331 per year, according to the Education Data Initiative. Over a four-year period, that's $141,324—and it doesn't include the cost of books or room and board! The prices have been rising and will continue to rise!

Investing your money to help pay for college is a smart financial decision. Your level of investment risk will depend on when you start college and when you start investing for it. The sooner you need access to your college money, the lower the risk tolerance you'll have when investing for your education.

Do Your Research

There are thousands of companies in the world in which you can you invest, but not all of them will be successful, climb to the top of their industry, or stay at the top forever! With so many companies available, it's important to do your research before investing. After all, this is your hard-earned money, so you want to make sure it's being put to good use!

If you've done your research, when the stock markets get choppy and stock prices go down, you'll know your reasons to hang on to your investments and you won't panic and sell out of fear. That is how many investors lose money.

FACTORS TO CONSIDER BEFORE INVESTING

The good thing about choosing companies is that the process can be very simple. Start with companies you already know. Here are five main factors you should consider before you invest in a company:

1. **Understand the business model:** It's one thing to be familiar with a product or a brand, but how does the company make money? How often do customers return? A company with a business model that has repeat customers is a good business model.

   Think about companies that you or your household make monthly payments to—software subscriptions, cell phones, or TV streaming services. Businesses that require customers to pay every month (a subscription-based model) are great because their revenues (income) are recurring and predictable. Look for this information in a company's Annual Report (also called the 10-K). This report can be found at the bottom of the company's website under "Investor Relations."

2. **Competitors:** Companies survive because they can protect their profits from their competitors.

   You can find who the competitors are in the Annual Report. Write down the competitors and think about whether these competitors stand a chance at "stealing" your company's customers. A company that is well-protected from competition has these features:

   ⇨ It offers something unique that people are willing to pay a lot of money for (think expensive, brand-name premium products).

   ⇨ Customers are unwilling to switch to a competitor, even if the competitor offers a lower price on a similar product.

3. **Revenue growth:** Has the company's revenue been growing over the past five years? More important, will it continue to grow? You can find this information on various finance websites or in the company's **financial statements** (also located under "Investor Relations")—specifically the profit and loss statement (P&L), which is also known as the **income statement**.

Financial statements that inform investors are published on a quarterly basis, so every three months. When a company reports its fourth quarter results, it also provides a full-year summary (annual financial statement).

4. **Gross margin:** How much does a company make from its products after materials and labor are accounted for?

Imagine a company that sells boats for $8,000 each. The boats are manufactured in Indonesia and the direct costs of making the boats include:

⇨ Raw materials

⇨ Labor costs

⇨ Transporting the finished boats

⇨ Warehouse storage

The direct cost of manufacturing one boat is $3,000. Therefore, the profit margin (the money made after direct costs are accounted for) is: $8,000 − $3,000 = $5,000 per boat.

Calculate the gross margin for each boat by dividing the profit margin by the sale price:

$5,000 (profit margin)/$8,000 (sale price) = 62.5% (gross margin)

Look for companies with high gross margins and compare their numbers to their competitors'. The higher the gross margin, the better!

5. **Earnings (net income):** Is the company profitable? After accounting for the direct costs of a business, there are other expenses as well—the **indirect costs**.

  Continuing with the boat example, the indirect costs of the business are:

→ Marketing and sales

→ Office rent

→ Staff salaries

→ General expenses

→ Taxes

  Let's say in 2023:

→ The company sold 1,000 boats, which is $8,000,000 in sales revenue.

→ Total direct costs amounted to $3,000,000.

→ Total indirect costs amount to $2,950,000.

  That means, the company generated a profit or **net income** of:

$8,000,000 − $3,000,000 − $2,950,000 = $2,050,000

The company made a profit! Ask yourself if they can continue growing their earnings (their net income)— either by selling more boats or increasing their prices.

YOU'RE NOT DONE YET!

Once you've made your initial investment into a company, you should continue to monitor it to make sure it stays on track with its revenue and earnings growth. You basically want to make sure they actually do what they say they'll do.

Will there be short-term hiccups? Absolutely! No business is perfect. As long as there is no fundamental change to the business—anything that will permanently affect their future products or services in a negative way—and it can keep its competitors from stealing business, the company should be able to survive and grow!

EXPERT TIP

Invest in what you know. The best investors in the world will say you need to understand and enjoy what you're researching. Think about what you like, what you wear, the products you use, and what surrounds you. Then make a list of those companies as a starting point.

GATHER YOUR DATA

Use the table on page 53 to record your investment research.

1. Pick a company you're interested in.

2. Go on the company's website and scroll all the way down to find the "Investor Relations" or "Investor Information" link.

3. Find the Annual Report (10-K) from the most recent full year. You can also look at the Investor Presentation. It gives a nice overview of the company. Jot down how the business generates sales and who their competitors are.

4. Go through the company's past income statements. You can find them on financial websites or EDGAR—the government site where all financial statements are filed every quarter, including the Annual Report (10-K).

5. In a spreadsheet, write down the company's past performance in revenue, gross margins, and net income over the past five years. Look for patterns of growth. Ideally, these numbers are improving over time.

6. Make a decision. Are you confident this company will be around for the next ten or twenty years, at least?

Company Name: _____	2019	2020	2021	2022	2023
Revenue ($)					
Revenue Growth Year-after-Year (%)					
Gross Profit ($)					
Gross Margins (%)					
Net Income ($)					
Growth in Net Income (%)					

Do you notice any growth patterns in revenue, gross margins, and net income? If yes, then you're onto something good!

Investing in Your Values

When you invest in a company, you become an owner of the company with many other owners. Think of it as having a slice of an enormous pie. When you own part of a company, you become a **shareholder**. As a shareholder, you are choosing to support the company's mission, their values, and how they conduct their business—good or bad.

For example, you might research a clothing company and then find it consumes a lot of water and energy and uses labor in developing countries because costs are low there. You may not be thrilled with the environmental footprint they're leaving behind or their labor practices. This company may not align with your values, and you may choose not to support them. This probably includes not investing in them. These days, investors are demanding more from companies and encouraging them to focus on more than just profits—including the environmental and social impact of running their business.

When choosing companies that align with your values, first select companies that interest you. Before you go digging into their financial statements, take a look at their website. Scroll all the way to the bottom and look for information related to sustainability, social impact, inclusion, diversity, culture, etc. This information may also be in their Investor Presentation. Find out what the company supports and if those things align with your values. It will become a part of your research when looking for companies to invest in.

As you do research, you may begin to sift out companies that are not acceptable to you. For example, some companies extract fossil fuels. You may decide you don't want to directly support them, and you may even stay away from the entire industry. These days, making a massive profit isn't the only priority. The investment industry has evolved to include a type of investing strategy (ESG) that addresses environmental impact, social responsibility, and good governance.

ESG INVESTING

ESG (environmental, social, and governance) investing is a strategy that factors in how well a company addresses those issues, in addition to making a profit for their investors. Businesses are graded by financial companies. This grade holds them accountable to their actions and ensures they're doing what they say they will when it comes to making a positive impact.

Environmental issues include how much greenhouse gas and waste a company produces, how much water and natural resources they use, and anything else that leaves an environmental footprint. Social issues address the well-being of everyone involved in the business, including the workers they employ (are they inclusive, diverse, and fair?) and the community that's impacted by the operations of the business. Pay equity and the impact the products have on people are also part of this.

Governance addresses the ethics of the company, including issues like how company executives are compensated, how much they spend on lobbying political parties, incidence of corruption and bribery, how successful the board of directors is at being independent and truly representing their investors, and how transparent management is to their investors when reporting the performance of the company.

These factors are important because businesses can get carried away and focus only on profits without much thought on the impact they'll have on people and the environment. Good governance is in place to ensure investors are protected and not defrauded, as we have witnessed in the past with companies like Enron.

Check Your Bottom Line

What you've learned in this chapter:

⇒ Why investing and starting early is a smart financial decision

⇒ The risks involved with investing and the rewards that come with it

⇒ How to determine your risk tolerance

⇒ How to start researching companies you want to invest in

⇒ How to invest in companies that align with your values

CHAPTER 4

Low-Risk Investments

Remember when I said there is no such thing as a free lunch? When we take big risks, we can make higher returns. If we invest in low-risk stuff, we receive lower returns. This chapter focuses on the various low-risk products available. They are important because the primary objective of low-risk investments is to preserve your **capital** (things of value, like money) while making small gains. As we discussed, money you need sooner rather than later is better invested in low-risk options.

There are varying degrees of risk within the category of low-risk investments. We will explore each investment in detail—treasury bills, certificates of deposit, and corporate bonds—and provide a risk level for each. A risk level of 1 is lowest and 10 is highest.

Treasury Bills

The lowest-risk investment you can make is lending money to the government. The government borrows money to fund public projects, like building roads and schools. In return for lending them money, you are promised interest payments and your original investment (the principal) back at a set point in the future (the maturity)—nothing more and nothing less. It is called debt security.

Treasury bills (T-bills) are considered one of the safest investments because:

→ They are backed by the U.S. government, so you're guaranteed to receive your principal.

→ Their maturity is generally one year or less.

→ They are exempt from state and local taxes (but not federal taxes).

→ You can cash them in anytime by selling them, making them very liquid investments.

T-bills are low-risk, so the interest rates are very low. Factors that make them low-risk are:

Zero default risk: The 100% guarantee of receiving your money back plus interest is backed by the U.S. government.

Maturity: The longer you must wait to receive your principal, the riskier it is for the borrower; therefore, you can expect higher interest rates. Treasury bills with long maturities pay higher interest rates.

When T-bills are sold, they are sold at a discount to par value. Par value is the amount promised to be repaid at maturity, and it could be as little as $100. The difference between the discounted purchase price and par value is the interest earned. For example, when you buy a $1,000 T-bill, you may purchase it for $950, a discount to par value. When it matures, you will receive the full par value of $1,000. The $50 difference is the interest earned.

SUCCESS STORY

So far, I have lived through three major recessions: the dot-com bubble burst in 2000, the Great Recession in 2008, and the coronavirus pandemic in 2020. Millions of people lost their jobs, companies went bankrupt, stock prices crashed, and people's investments lost a lot of value—up to 40% during the Great Recession. The greatest risk during these times was being 100% invested in the stock markets.

Those who were invested only in U.S. Treasuries or were holding cash in their certificates of deposit (CDs) escaped these major losses completely (unless their CD was held at a bank that went bankrupt). Those who invested only a portion of their portfolio in low-risk investments lost less money. People in both these groups were considered winners. That's because during times like these, people tend to move toward low-risk investments like the ones discussed in this chapter. This practice ultimately drives up the prices of these low-risk investments because of the increased demand.

Certificates of Deposit

| 1 | 2 | 3 | 4 | 5 | 6 | 7 | 8 | 9 | 10 | **RISK LEVEL 2** |

Another type of investment that pays you interest is a certificate of deposit (CD). They are similar to Treasury bills, but CDs are issued by banks and credit unions. When you deposit money in a bank account, you're basically loaning the bank money. Remember, the function of a bank is to lend money and store money deposits. The more money that is deposited, the more money it can lend out!

The bank or credit union will pay you a higher interest rate for a CD than for a regular savings account because you must leave the deposit alone until it matures. Your money is locked in for a fixed period, and if you with-draw it early, you will get penalized—typically by losing some of the interest payment.

You can select CDs with maturities anywhere from three months to five years (even ten years, but that's not a good use of your money).

CDs are considered low-risk because:

⇨ You are guaranteed to get your money back plus interest.

⇨ They are liquid—if the CD has no penalty when it is withdrawn.

⇨ They offer various maturities, both short-term and long-term.

Note that the **default risk** here is slightly higher than with the T-bills because banks can fail and not repay their debts, whereas the U.S. government has never in its entire history defaulted on their debt. The guarantee is only as good as the issuer, and in this case, deposits with banks are generally safe.

CDs typically have a minimum deposit requirement and interest is paid either monthly, quarterly, yearly, or at maturity. They will vary depending on the CD issued by the bank or credit union.

HOW TO GET STARTED WITH CDS

With CDs, it's all about shopping around each bank and credit union to see which one offers the highest rates. Each bank or credit union website will provide information on the CDs they offer, such as:

⇨ How much interest you'll receive, quoted in annual percentage yield (APY)

⇨ The various maturities offered (six months, two years, five years, etc.)

➡ When you'll receive these interest payments (monthly, quarterly, yearly, etc.)

➡ Any penalties for early withdrawal

➡ The minimum deposit required

➡ Any maintenance fees

You can check out blogs that provide a comparison of the highest CD rates across the country—but they can be limited to the big banks. You may have a credit union in your neighborhood that's not listed and possibly offering a good CD rate. As such, you will need an adult to assist you with this process if you are under eighteen years old.

SHOPPING FOR CDS

CDs are one of the safest places to store your money, so they can be used as a vehicle to protect your money in the short term while earning a bit more interest than a savings account.

Do an online search for the best CD rates you can find and include any credit unions in your local area to make sure you get the best rate. Keep in mind you can't touch any money you put into a CD for a specified time—if you do, you'll pay a penalty.

Bank/Credit Union	Interest Rate (APY)	Term of CD (6 months)

What Is a Credit Rating?

A random stranger asks to borrow money from you. Your best friend asks to borrow money from you. Who would you trust more to pay you back? Obviously, your best friend (I hope!) because you know and trust them. But how can you assess institutions when you lend them money?

Credit agencies evaluate the financial strength of companies and governments. They give them a grade, called a credit rating, that determines how trustworthy they are to make their interest payments and principal repayments on time. S&P Global Ratings, Moody's, DBRS Morningstar, and Fitch Group are the four main agencies, and each has its own grading system.

On the following page is a summary of the four agencies and their grading systems. The higher the grade, the lower the risk, and the lower the returns an investor should expect. The red middle line divides the debt into two categories: investment-grade bonds (low risk) and high-yield bonds (high risk).

Investment-Grade Bonds	S&P	Fitch	Moody's	DBRS
Low Risk **Low Returns**	AAA	AAA	Aaa	AAA
	AA+	AA+	Aa1	AA (high)
	AA	AA	Aa2	AA
	AA-	AA-	Aa3	AA (low)
	A+	A+	A1	A (high)
	A	A	A2	A
	A-	A-	A3	A (low)
	BBB+	BBB+	Baa1	BBB (high)
	BBB	BBB	Baa2	BBB
	BBB-	BBB-	Baa3	BBB (low)
High-Yield Bonds	BB+	BB+	Ba1	BB (high)
High Risk **High Returns**	BB	BB	Ba2	BB
	BB-	BB-	Ba3	BB (low)
	B+	B+	B1	B (high)
	B	B	B2	B
	B-	B-	B3	B (low)
	CCC+	CCC+	Caa1	CCC (high)
	CCC	CCC	Caa2	CCC
	CCC-	CCC-	Caa3	CCC (low)
	D	D		D

MONEY MATTERS: WHEN SHOULD YOU INVEST IN BONDS?

I mentioned briefly in chapter 3 (page 40) that bonds are low-risk, low-return investments compared with stocks. That's because bonds are a debt security where the investor expects interest payments and their principal upon maturity—nothing more and nothing less. Bonds, including Treasury bills and CDs, are a form of debt security where the payments are predictable and less than exciting. So why would anyone invest in them, you ask?

Bonds are a good option when:

◇ You would like income and are willing to sacrifice growth. (Remember Jane? She didn't know she was sacrificing growth.) Remember the income will not make up for the gains and profits you'd get from investing in stocks.

◇ You don't want your portfolio's value to fluctuate a lot with the stock markets. This process is called volatility.

Investment-Grade Bonds

 **RISK LEVEL 3**

Did you know some companies have better credit ratings than the U.S. government? It's true! Ratings change over time. The U.S. government wasn't always sitting at AA+ (the second-highest rating). It was downgraded from AAA back in 2011 because of the high levels of debt. There is no need to worry, though, because the U.S. government has unlimited amounts of money. But *how*?

Everyone has a borrowing limit—including the U.S. government, sort of. The maximum amount of money the U.S. government is allowed to borrow is determined by the debt ceiling—the maximum amount of money it can borrow through bonds—but the U.S. government also controls what this debt ceiling is! The government has raised its debt ceiling numerous times in the past, which allows it to continue borrowing money (issuing bonds) from investors all over the world. This is how they've never defaulted on any of their debt obligations in the past (they were close at one point, but it didn't happen).

Likewise, some companies are also considered very safe and, much like the government, can be quite boring. They are not your typical up-and-coming, high-growth companies that boast all over social media. There is nothing thrilling about these highly rated companies. That's because their high-growth periods are over and they have matured into stable, financially strong entities that:

→ Are profitable enough to provide a predictable income stream for their debt and even **equity** investors

→ Are unlikely to fail to make their payments

→ Can navigate through difficult times

As a result, they can take advantage of their high ratings by borrowing money to fund their projects—and pay low interest rates to their debt investors.

HOW TO GET STARTED

The best way to invest in bonds is to invest in a whole bunch of them at the same time—not just a bond issued by one company. This is where **funds** come in. A fund is a pool of money that's invested in hundreds or even thousands of companies. They can be stocks, bonds, or both. A bond fund may contain hundreds of different types of investment-grade bonds from various companies or different levels of governments, like federal, state, and municipal.

When looking to invest in bonds, pay attention to the **coupon** (the potential interest payment you'll be paid). The information displayed on a bond fund's website will show you the average coupon you can expect to get. Keep in mind an adult is required to help you open your investment account when buying your investments.

High-Yield Bonds

 **RISK LEVEL 5**

We are moving up the risk ladder! Now we'll look at
bonds below the red line in the credit-rating chart—the
high-yield bonds. As the name suggests, these bonds
yield higher returns than investment-grade bonds
because the companies that issue them have a higher
risk profile, but they are still considered low-risk relative
to the investment options in the next chapter.

These types of bonds have high default risk because:

➡ They are not as stable and profitable.

➡ They have no history of credit. These companies are
issuing bonds for the first time, so there's no way to
tell if they will pay on time.

Because of these risks, investors must be compensated with a higher coupon rate.

When I worked in investment banking, I was involved in a deal to help a mining development company raise $100 million in debt to build their gold project. This company had a high-risk profile because:

- ➜ They had zero revenue because they'd spent years looking for metals and creating a plan to dig them out.

- ➜ It would take several years to build the project before they could sell their first ounce of gold.

- ➜ There was risk in constructing the project, like delays, running out of money, potential labor issues, etc.

- ➜ Gold prices are dictated by the markets.

Because of their high-risk profile, the company offered a $1,000 bond with a coupon that was close to 14% per year—in addition to giving investors an extra $50 above par value ($1,050) when it matured!

Remember that companies' financial positions change over time, so their credit ratings will change as well.

RISING STARS

Some companies may be issuing debt for the first time (like the gold company I mentioned), so there's no way to assess their credit worthiness. They can't prove to investors they will make their debt payments on time. Even if a company is financially strong with good revenue and profitability, without credit history, investors will demand higher yields. A company must earn their credit experience before they can be given a better grade.

A company that is headed in a good direction with potential for a lot of growth is able to attract investors. Over time, as it proves to everyone that it can make payments on time and continue to grow (the company and profits), its credit rating will improve. It can move above the red credit-rating line—hence the name, rising star.

FALLING ANGELS

As the name suggests, these companies were once investment-grade (above the red line), but have since been downgraded because of their change in financial stability. Declining revenues or other financial issues that may hinder their ability to make their debt obligations is enough to cause a downgrade from the credit-rating agencies.

For example, Company X once dominated an entire market and enjoyed ten years of stability, earning massive profits for its shareholders and an A rating from S&P. Eventually a competitor, Company Y, entered the market and started stealing market shares with their new technology. Over several years, with declining revenues and lack of innovation to compete, Company X's profits suffered. The future of the company was in question, so S&P downgraded them from A- to BB. Now, as Company X tries to issue debt, they'll have to pay higher coupon rates.

JUNK BONDS

A company that issues junk bonds does not imply the company is junk! They are called junk bonds simply because they are not investment grade, so these companies are all below the red line. There are varying levels of statuses and names, which is why names like rising stars and falling angels were created. Junk bonds have a high risk of defaulting, so they have high yields to help mitigate the risk to the investor.

HOW TO GET STARTED

Much like investing in investment-grade bonds, the easiest way to invest in high-yield bonds is through a fund. As you research bond funds, you will see by their titles if they are high-yield bonds or investment-grade bonds.

The beauty of investing in funds and not just individual bonds or stocks is being diversified—having your money in many different places. By investing in a fund and gaining exposure to hundreds of different types of bonds, you won't lose all your money if a few companies default on their payments. Bond funds are also more accessible for investors with small amounts of money, because companies that issue bonds may require minimum amounts of $1,000 or more, as opposed to no minimum for some bond funds.

Assess whether this would be suitable for your portfolio. As always, consult with an adult to help you with the process before you decide to invest.

DETERMINE HOW MUCH YOU WANT TO INVEST IN BONDS

Let's calculate the potential results of having bonds in your portfolio! Say you invest 50% of your money in bonds that pay on average 2.5% per year in interest, and the other 50% in stocks. Let's say you can earn a potential return of 10% in the stock markets. You'd expect to earn an average of (10 + 2.5)/2 = 6.25% per year with this strategy. Alternatively, if you had invested 100% of your money in stocks, you would have earned 10% on your money.

Now let's say the stock markets have a bad year and you earn –5%: That's a loss for the year. You'd still earn 2.5% in interest payments on 50% of your portfolio invested in bonds. If we average the stock's loss against the bonds' gain, your overall portfolio would only be down –1.25%, as opposed to –5% if you were 100% invested in stocks. So are you willing to sacrifice growth for safety? Can you tolerate these potential downturns in the stock markets? Crunch some numbers like we did above and see what you're willing to tolerate.

Check Your Bottom Line

What you've learned in this chapter:

⮞ When you'll need low-risk investments in your portfolio

⮞ What Treasury bills are and why they are riskless

⮞ What certificates of deposit are and their uses

⮞ What credit ratings are and who provides them

⮞ The differences between investment-grade and high-yield bonds

CHAPTER 5

High-Risk Investments

What was the scariest thing you've wanted to do, but then you backed out because of fear? Maybe you wanted to try out for the school basketball team, but you didn't because you didn't think you were tall enough. Or maybe you wanted to ask your crush out on a date, but you didn't want to get rejected—and now they're dating someone else!

See how *not* taking risks can affect the glorious outcomes, no matter how scary the process? Imagine you tried out for the team, and now you're on the starting lineup. You asked your crush out and now you're dating. Investing is no different. When you take risks, you can be rewarded with great returns.

This chapter focuses on high-risk investments, specifically, the different types of equity: public company stocks, private equity, real estate, and angel investing. As in the previous chapter, each investment will be given a risk rating—1 is the lowest risk and 10 is the highest. Let's start with stocks.

The Stock Market

RISK LEVEL 6-8

If you've ever strolled through the downtown areas of major cities like New York, Los Angeles, or London you've probably noticed a lot of high-powered people (mostly men) in fancy suits walking super fast while on their cell phones. Chances are they work in finance. This scene is very common on Wall Street in Manhattan, where the New York Stock Exchange is—one of the largest financial centers of the world.

We're going to look at two common functions of Wall Street: trading stocks for investors and raising capital for companies. But first, what is a stock and what is the stock market?

Stock: A stock is a fractional share of ownership in a company. When we talk about stocks as investments, we are referring to stocks of publicly traded companies. Publicly traded companies are companies that have stocks that are available to the public—like you, me, and anyone else on this planet. Private companies, on the other hand, don't have stocks available for everyone to own.

When you invest in stocks, you own shares of a company. For example, if you buy one share of ABC company, you become a shareholder of ABC company and are entitled to the profits they pay out—if they pay them out.

Stock Market: The stock market is a place (used to be physical, but now everything is done electronically) where stocks of all publicly traded companies are bought and sold. When we refer to the stock market, we are talking about a lot of companies— thousands all at once. These companies can be grouped into categories that collectively represent something. It is called an **index**.

One example is the S&P 500 index—a group of the 500 largest publicly traded companies in the United States. Together they are a representation (indicator) of the U.S. economy. Companies like Alphabet (Google), Apple, Amazon, Walmart, and Disney are part of this index (along with 495 other companies). Together they generate trillions of dollars in revenue and employ millions of Americans. Likewise, the Dow Jones Industrial Average (DJIA) contains thirty major companies in the United States from various industries. Collectively the Dow represents the U.S. economy as well.

How much should I pay for a stock?

When completing the company research we discussed in chapter 3, you must make sure you're not buying a company's stock just because everyone else is buying it. The stock price may be pushed way higher than it should be (called overvaluation) simply because of the increased demand.

Stock prices are determined by their **fair market value**, which is the value of a company based on its future projected earnings. There are tons of people on Wall Street who make these calculations, so stocks are always theoretically trading at a fair value. Unfortunately, it is not always the case because stock prices are driven primarily by supply and demand. It's why research is important. You need your own reasons to invest in the stocks you choose, and to ensure you're not overpaying.

STOCKS VS. GAMBLING

So how is this different from gambling at the casino or playing the lottery if there's a risk of losing money in stocks? Why don't I just buy lottery tickets in hopes of hitting the jackpot, or take my chances at the casino and try to win fast money?

Because the odds are *not* in your favor when you gamble.

When you're investing in stocks, you are taking a calculated risk and implementing a proven strategy where the odds of making money increase in your favor when you invest in good companies and the longer you stay invested.

Each time you gamble or play the lottery, you either win or you lose. When you lose, the money is gone forever with no chance for you to recuperate that loss—unless you put more money in and play again.

When investing, you can watch the value of your stocks go down, but it's not a locked-in loss. There's a chance of the investment recovering—and you're still receiving dividends (more on dividends later)!

BEAR MARKET

Individual companies' stock prices can crash big time, likely because of poor performance or poor future outlook. When it happens to the stock markets overall and there is a prolonged decline in stock prices that total 20% or more because of negative investor emotions, the stock market is in a **bear market**. Stock prices are based on the future projected earnings of companies, so stock prices are driven down when people become pessimistic about companies' prospects.

Bear markets can last for several weeks, months, or even decades. In March 2020, U.S. stock markets entered a bear market triggered by the COVID-19 pandemic. From February 19, 2020 (when the stock market hit its all-time high), to March 23, 2020, the S&P 500 index dropped 34% in value—wiping out three years' worth of gains! This situation is called a bear market because of how a bear attacks its prey—with its claws swiping downward.

BULL MARKET

The opposite of a bear market is a **bull market**, when stock prices rise at least 20% over a prolonged period because of positive investor emotions, which is when investors are very optimistic about the future. During the 2020 pandemic, as news of successful vaccines were released, people became more confident and certain of the future. It meant the return to normalcy.

On March 19, 2021, one year after the stock market hit its lowest point, S&P 500 index investors enjoyed a whopping 70% gain on their stocks.

The COVID-19 pandemic created one of the shortest bear markets in history. Just as quickly as prices collapsed in early 2020, they recovered in record time. You can imagine a bull attacking with its horns in an upward motion—symbolizing the increase in stock prices.

BLACK SWAN EVENTS

The COVID-19 pandemic seemed like it came out of nowhere and felt very unpredictable. But it wasn't our first pandemic—there was the Spanish flu pandemic of 1918—and it certainly won't be our last. Black swan events are unexpected and unprecedented, and result in severe and widespread consequences. The September 11, 2001, attacks on the World Trade Center in New York City were a black swan event. The stock markets closed for four days after the attacks, and the S&P 500 index lost almost 12% in value over several days of trading after reopening.

Black swan events are impossible to predict, so they should not impact your overall investment strategy. It is why the money allocated toward your stock investment is for your long-term goals—so it has time to recover from bear markets and even black swan events. The name "black swan" is derived from the Western belief that all swans are white. Any black swans were considered an anomaly.

RECESSION OR DEPRESSION?

I graduated college in 2008—at the peak of the Great Recession. I was unemployed for more than ten months—along with thirty million Americans who lost their jobs during the period between December

S&P 500 INDEX
1970–2021

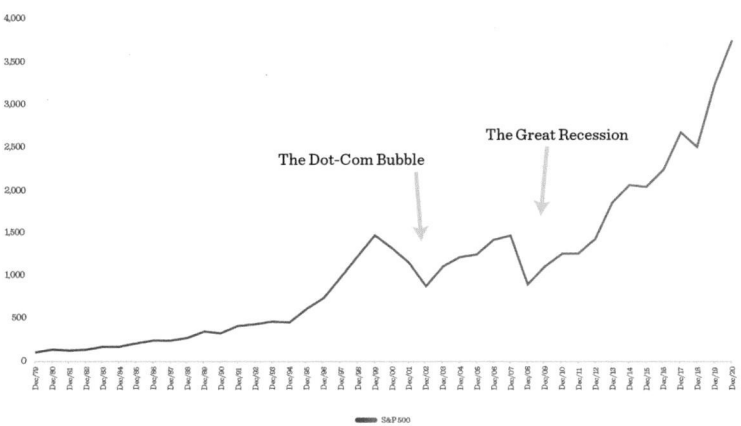

The Dot-Com Bubble

The Great Recession

S&P 500

2007 and June 2009. The S&P 500 index had lost almost 40% in value from the peak to trough (see chart above). More than $10 trillion in investment portfolios and home values were wiped out.

In a recession, the economy struggles with job losses and reduced incomes. It results in fewer sales for companies (which impact stock prices directly). The country overall makes less money as they sell fewer goods. It is measured by the **real gross domestic product (real GDP)**. Although economists have many definitions for a recession, it can generally be defined as two consecutive quarters of declines in real GDP.

A depression is a more severe version of a recession, usually lasting years. The Great Depression, which lasted from 1929 to 1939, was the worst economic downturn in U.S. history. It began when the stock market crashed in 1929 (down 89%!). The crash was followed by millions of jobs lost and half of America's banks failing.

The United States has recovered from every recession and depression because governments intervene by lowering interest rates to stabilize the economy. This practice encourages companies to borrow money to invest in their businesses and hire people. It also gets people to borrow money to spend on products and services. It's important to be aware of what's happening in the economy so you can brace yourself on what to expect with your investments.

HOW TO BUY STOCKS

Once you've done your research on the companies you want to invest in, it's time to execute! Buying stocks is a similar process to opening a savings account except with a few more steps. If you're under eighteen years old, you'll need an adult with you to open an account.

1. **Choose a brokerage company to open an account with.** A brokerage company is a financial institution that acts like a middleman connecting buyers and sellers of **securities**, like stocks. Prior to the digital world, investors would have to call someone at the brokerage (a broker) to purchase or sell their stocks. Today people can use online platforms to open accounts and buy and sell securities on their own without speaking to anyone.

2. **Select the type of account to open.** If you're under eighteen years old, you'll need a parent or guardian to open an account on your behalf. It is a custodial

account, and your parent/guardian will have control over it until you turn eighteen years old (or twenty-one in some states).

If you have earned income, your parent or guardian can open a custodial Roth IRA account (IRA stands for individual retirement account) for you. A Roth IRA has these features:

➔ Your investments grow tax-free and money you withdraw after retirement is tax-free.

➔ There are annual limits on how much you can contribute to this account. In 2024, the maximum amount you can put into this account is $7,000. If you earned only $3,000 for the year, however, $3,000 would be your maximum allowable contribution.

➔ If you earn more than a certain amount in a given year (in 2024 the threshold is $161,000), you'll no longer qualify to contribute money to this account.

➔ A custodial Roth IRA allows you to withdraw your contributions (money you deposit, not earned income) tax-free. You won't be able to do so once you have full control over the account and it becomes a regular Roth IRA.

Max out your Roth IRA to take full advantage of the tax-free growth on your investments. After a certain income level, you will no longer be eligible to use a Roth IRA for your investments—and all investments will be fully taxable!

If you don't have earned income, you may open a regular custodial brokerage account that is fully taxable on all earnings.

Another type of account you can open is a youth account. Teens who are thirteen to seventeen years old can control the account and allow parents to monitor the activity and transactions. Not all brokerages offer a youth account, so you'll need to do a little online shopping.

3. **Fund your account.** Once you've opened your account, it's time to put money in it! You can make a deposit into your investment account by linking it to your checking or savings account.

4. **Buy your first stock.** Once your account is funded, it's time to buy your first stock! After you have selected the stocks you want, find out what the ticker symbol is for each company. The ticker symbol is unique to the company, like a student number. A simple search online of "XYZ company ticker symbol" should do the trick. Amazon's ticker symbol is AMZN, for example.

Once you've purchased the stocks, make sure you check on them every few months to make sure the company stays on track with their growth plans.

DIVIDENDS

Dividends are profits paid out (usually four times a year) by companies as a reward to their shareholders. Usually, companies that have been around for a while are the ones giving dividends to their investors. A common misconception is that dividend companies are boring because they are mature companies that don't grow a lot in stock price. Not true!

Some companies pump out so much cash simply because they are superior businesses. They can afford to pay investors dividends *and* grow their company! In turn, they also reward shareholders with **capital gains**, which are stock price gains. These companies are the real winners because their stock investors have two ways to earn money: dividends *and* capital gains. Because dividends are generally paid quarterly, you'll see cash flow into your account four times a year from these types of companies.

For example, ABC company has been paying its shareholders dividends for the past ten years. They declared a dividend of $1.40 per share for the most recent quarter. If you owned 25 shares of ABC company, you'd be paid $1.40 × 20 = $28. If they pay every quarter, you can potentially earn $112 in a year!

Companies with a history of growing and paying dividends have proven to outperform companies that do not pay dividends, so be sure to add some of these to your portfolio and reinvest the money you receive! Dividends may even boost your confidence as an investor because you get to see a noticeable benefit within a short period of time after investing your money.

I made my first investment when I was twenty years old. I picked a company that was on the brink of bankruptcy, so I lost money. Clearly I didn't do my research! I lost a bit of confidence, but it didn't deter me from investing.

After paying off my credit card debt, I started investing in the stock markets. I invested in a combination of dividend-paying companies and high-risk companies (called resource exploration companies) that generated no cash flow. Resource exploration companies can be tricky because they are part of a very technical industry and don't generate cash flow, and their success depends on the discovery of resources like gold, copper, and oil to increase their stock prices.

I worked with many resource exploration companies, which is how I gained my knowledge in this industry. Before I turned thirty years old, I had built an investment portfolio worth more than $100,000—which gave me a lot of options when I lost my job. I felt secure, wasn't worried about my bills, and was not pressured to find a new job.

WHEN TO SELL

Of course, when you're investing, you're looking to make a profit. That's why it makes sense to buy a stock at a low price, then sell it later for a higher price. Buy low, sell high: as simple as it sounds, it's not always easy to do. It's natural for investors' fear to kick in during bear markets or recessionary times as they watch the value of their portfolios go down.

Here are the rules I use to figure out when to sell a stock:

1. When you need the money. The time will come to cash out your investments to pay for your college education or whatever goal you had set.

2. When the company you invested in is no longer on track with their plans because of a major change to their business—like a new competitor stealing a lot of their customers or a new government regulation that directly affects how they run their business.

3. When there is a better investment opportunity somewhere else.

Because you're largely investing for the long term, you won't need to sell a lot. I don't sell a lot. Some of the most successful investors hold on to their investments for decades at a time, giving companies the chance to grow and execute their vision.

When selling, you can choose to sell the stocks that made you the most money first. If you bought ABC stock for $30 per share, and it's now at $55, you made a capital gain of $55 – $30 = $25 per share, or an 83% return on your money. Do this exercise to see which shares made you the highest return on a percentage basis. Keep in mind you will need to pay taxes on those returns (more on this later!).

YOUR FIRST INVESTMENT

Ready to open your investment account? It's as easy as 1, 2, 3, 4!

Step One. Talk to your parent/guardian about opening up your investment account. They may already have accounts with a specific brokerage and will likely set yours up in the same place.

Step Two. If your parent/guardian does not have an account with a specific brokerage company, do some online research to see which brokerages offer custodial accounts. Not all brokerages offer them, so you'll have to choose one that does.

Step Three. Choose the type of investment account you want. Again, if you have earned income, I highly recommend a custodial Roth IRA to take advantage of the tax-free growth of your investments. Note that if your account has been open for more than five years you can make tax-free withdrawals for qualified education expenses and withdraw up to $10,000 to buy your first house.

Step Four. Fund the account with the money you want to invest.

You're ready to go!

Private Equity

| 1 | 2 | 3 | 4 | 5 | 6 | 7 | 8 | 9 | 10 | **RISK LEVEL 8** |

I mentioned the differences between a publicly traded company and a private company at the beginning of this chapter. You know you can invest in public companies through the stock market, but is it possible to invest in private companies, too? Yes, but not for you. Before a company goes public, chances are they have private investors who fund their growth and operations. These private investors are often private funds, hence the name private equity.

Investing in private businesses is out of reach for average investors like you and me. Those investments are reserved for what are called accredited investors, who are experienced and have a lot of money. These accredited investors invest in private equity funds. The managers of those funds then invest in the businesses on their behalf. Private equity funds usually require investors to write checks of at least $250,000.

When a company needs money to grow their business, they have two options: through private investors or public investors. When you buy stocks, you're not giving the company any money. You're buying the stock from another current owner, who is willing to sell you their shares for a certain price. When a company needs money, they will need to issue new shares. Let's illustrate this with a pie example.

Imagine a pie (the company) divided into eight slices. There are eight pie owners in total and you own one of the slices. That means you own ⅛ or 12.5% of the pie. When a company raises money to fund their operations, that money comes in from new investors. The pie just got bigger because it just got some money, but now there are sixteen owners instead of eight, so your slice just got smaller. You now own only 6% of the company. This process is called dilution.

When a company receives money through a private equity fund, the business is still at a high-risk stage. Therefore, these funds will demand a higher percentage ownership of the company. The investors may even be involved with the company's operations to help it out. The fund may bring in a new management team or introduce the company to a new customer base with their connections. It becomes a strategic investment and not just a financial investment (which is what stocks are).

Private equity is considered an alternative to investing in the stock markets because:

→ Private companies are not subjected to stock price fluctuations caused by buyer and seller activity in the public markets. This positive benefit is a major reason businesses choose to stay private.

→ Private companies are illiquid because investors cannot just cash out easily. They have to find another private investor or wait until the company goes public to sell their ownership position. It's the cost of investing in private businesses.

Private businesses escape the strict requirements of being public. They are not required to provide quarterly earnings reports, don't have to be transparent with their financials, and don't have to deal with Wall Street and their potential scrutiny! These are some reasons companies choose to stay private.

MONEY MATTERS: WHY COMPANIES GO PUBLIC

Why do companies go public? There are several reasons, including:

◇ It allows their private shareholders to cash out and lets them find new buyers in a public offering.

◇ They can raise capital outside of private investors by attracting a new investor base.

◇ They have too many shareholders. At a certain point, the law requires them to go public and report their financials.

Going Public on a Stock Exchange

When a company goes public, they invite people to own shares of their company. It's called the Initial Public Offering (IPO). The IPO can be done in one of two ways:

Primary Offering: The company attracts new investors to raise capital to fund the company.

Secondary Offering: Current shareholders of the private company (e.g., private equity investors) sell their shares to new investors. The company doesn't raise any new money because it's essentially just an ownership swap.

Venture Capital

Before I founded my company and became an author, I worked for a venture capital (VC) fund company. My job was to assess businesses the fund wanted to invest in. I was the only employee working with the two founders of the company. I learned a lot about this business over a short period of time.

The two founders of the VC pooled together their own money, gathered other investors, and started a VC fund worth about $50 million. The founders' job was to use the $50 million to invest in private businesses that were in a high-risk stage—often when they were just starting to generate their first $5 million in revenue.

The VC provided capital to these businesses that would allow them to expand their operations. They could invest in marketing, hire new people, expand their production lines—or anything else that would help the company generate revenue many times over their current income. The risk to the VC is high at this point because the business is private, so the investment is not liquid and there's no guarantee the business will be successful. If the business fails, the VC's entire investment is lost.

If the business flourishes, however, and its annual revenue goes from $5 million to $25 million, the VC investment just made a five-fold return on their

High-Risk Investments   **97**

investment! The expectation is that growth happens in a short period of time, typically within several years.

Venture capital investing is higher risk than private-equity investments because VCs invest at a point when the company is just starting to generate revenue. In this case, their investments would earn a bigger slice of the pie—often up to half of the company's ownership.

If you ever watch the show *Shark Tank*, you'll see a panel of **venture capitalists** (the sharks) listening to entrepreneurs pitch their businesses, in hopes of attracting money to fund their growth. These investors are considered sharks because when companies are in a desperate position, they can be taken advantage of. The sharks often take a higher percentage of ownership than the entrepreneur wants to give up.

Imagine you spent three years building a business on your own. Then a new investor comes in, writes you a check, and now owns half your business! Venture capitalists offer more than just a financial investment, though. Like private equity investors, they offer expertise, connections, and other value-added items that can benefit the business beyond just money.

START IT UP!

Imagine you and a friend have an idea for a technology business. You poured your savings into the company and have some revenue coming in, but you're not yet profitable. At this point, to keep the business going, you'll need to hire some employees—perhaps several new developers and some sales and marketing people. You have a start-up! Start-ups are very common in technology and often attract venture capitalists because:

→ If the technology is successful, whether it's an app or new product, the potential returns can be magnificent. Many millionaires and billionaires were created because they invested at this stage of the business.

→ The largest companies in the world are technology companies, and there is potential for those giants to acquire start-ups. They often pay very high prices and make investors and the founders massive returns on their investments.

Many businesses fail because of lack of funding. They simply can't conduct business without capital, which is why venture capitalists play a critical role in helping businesses move forward. The risk to investors is substantial because there's still a chance, even with funding, that the business will fail. At this stage of the business, companies are not profitable because they are taking on a lot of costs to build the company, but are not generating a lot of revenue. It's much different from a lot of the stocks you may have on your list that you'd want to invest in.

Real Estate Investments

 **RISK LEVEL 6**

Real estate investments involve buying a property and then renting it out to generate monthly income, or buying it and selling it at a higher price. One of the best decisions I made as a university student was buying a house and renting out the extra rooms to students. Doing so allowed me to live rent-free because the other students were paying my mortgage. It was a great investment, but it required a lot of work and money. I had to:

- ⇨ Work out all the costs of buying a house and the cost of ownership.

- ⇨ Figure out what to charge students to make sure the rental income covered all the costs.

- ⇨ Find a house that was in my price range that was in a good location and desirable for students.

- ⇨ Pool money together for a down payment. (My parents helped by taking a loan against their home, which is called a home equity loan.)

- ⇨ Hire a real estate agent to help me shop for a house and put in offers.

- ⇨ Draft rental agreements and read about the laws between landlord and tenants.

There are a lot of risks involved in owning a rental property, such as:

⮕ Tenants not paying their rent or trashing the property

⮕ Increasing costs, like property taxes, condo fees, or the interest on the mortgage

⮕ Failure to find tenants to rent the property

⮕ Falling property values

⮕ Costly repairs if something breaks or is damaged

You must make payments on the property regardless of whether it is full of tenants, which can reduce your overall profits. This risk is why setting aside money is highly recommended.

If you're buying a house without the intention of renting it out (or living in it), you'll want to sell it as quickly as possible. It's called property flipping. This type of investment usually involves purchasing a house that's not in the best condition and renovating it to improve it so you can sell it for more than you bought it for.

Other types of real estate investments include owning a commercial building and renting it out to businesses or owning apartments and renting out units to families.

Other Physical Investments

 **RISK LEVEL 7**

Besides real estate, there are other types of physical investments, such as:

⮕ Art

⮕ Collectible cards (Pokémon, baseball, etc.)

- Antiques

- Comic books

- Limited edition toys

- Digital assets (which are not really physical!)

These investments are generally born out of hobbies. You definitely have to research which items are valuable. Not everything will appreciate (gain value). Things appreciate because of their popularity and the demand for the item. Scarcity of an item can increase its value. For example, there is only one *Mona Lisa* painting in the world. In 1962, the painting was worth $100 million—which is more than $800 million in today's dollars once **inflation** is factored in!

A new type of collectible has surfaced recently—NFTs. NFT stands for **non-fungible token**, which is a unique unit of data (like a digital certificate) stored online using something called blockchain technology. Cryptocurrency was born on the **blockchain**. Using this same technology, a new class of digital assets was born. These digital assets can be images, audios, or video clips.

NFTs emerged in popularity in 2021, paving a new way for artists to sell their work. Instead of selling physical artwork, they can sell digital art where ownership is confirmed and stored on the blockchain. Much like physical art, NFTs can be replicated and sold as authentic to those who are not familiar with this asset. You have to take caution and do a lot of research prior to investing. There have already been numerous scams in the marketplace.

Angel Investing

Before a start-up receives venture capital funding, other investors likely funded the business. They are called angel investors—very rich individuals who are willing to take the highest investment risk with businesses that are in their earliest stage. Their product or service may not even be developed yet—it could be just an idea or a concept.

For example, let's say you have a business idea and need to file some patents, but you don't have enough money to go through the process. You pitch your business idea to your rich uncle. He agrees to make a personal investment in your company and ends up owning 20% of your business.

At this stage, the product hasn't even been developed yet, so there is no revenue. He understands that in the future there will be additional investors funding the business until it's profitable, so his 20% ownership will be reduced (diluted).

Angel investors are often friends or family. This relationship means the conditions are not as difficult—unlike venture capital funds, which may attach strict requirements like minimum ownership or having certain people as a part of the company's management team.

RESEARCH YOUR NEXT NON-STOCK INVESTMENT

Besides stocks, brainstorm a few other types of investments. If you're interested in buying a house someday, crunch some numbers to see how much would be required to make the initial purchase. Give yourself a timeline so you'll know whether to save or invest. If you're looking to buy a house in ten years, you will need to invest for that purchase!

If you're interested in buying something like digital artwork in the form of an NFT, start doing research about how NFTs work, what makes them popular, and how to protect yourself in the digital space. Consider what sort of long-term value it can bring you and if it'll appreciate in the future. Write your notes below!

_____

_____

_____

_____

_____

_____

_____

Check Your Bottom Line

What you've learned in this chapter:

⇒ What the stock market is and how it works

⇒ How to buy stocks and know when to sell them

⇒ What's involved with investing in young businesses

⇒ The roles of venture capital, private equity funds, and angel investors

⇒ Physical investments like real estate and art

CHAPTER 6

Diversifying Your Funds

My first investment was with one company—and I watched their stock plummet over the course of a few months. Not only was it a terrible stock to begin with (it was an airline company that was on the brink of bankruptcy), but it was also my only investment. Because I didn't diversify, I watched my $200 shrink to pretty much nothing, and that was that. I didn't know what I was doing.

Successful investing isn't anything like what I did—picking one company, sticking with it, and then forgetting about it. On the flip side, diversification *is* a successful strategy. It's when you hold stocks in multiple companies just in case one or several companies go down. It's important to diversify with both a variety of companies and investment products.

In this chapter, we'll discuss how to diversify your investments, what the most successful investment strategy is, which investments take the least effort, and how to avoid losing all your money when investing.

How to Diversify

There's a saying: "Don't put all your eggs in one basket" (just in case you drop the basket and break everything). In investing, it means you should spread out your risk, in case one investment doesn't work out. This way, you still have the other ones keeping your money secure and (hopefully) growing.

Had I diversified my first investment, instead of holding just one company, I would have:

→ Earned much more money

→ Not lost confidence in investing

I simply didn't know how to invest or diversify my investments with the little money I had. Investing in two or three companies would have been better than just holding one company. But I didn't have many options back then or even close to the amount of information that's available today.

The best way to diversify is to invest in funds. As explained earlier, a fund is a pool of money that's invested in a whole bunch of products—like stocks and bonds. Investing in funds makes it much easier for people to get exposure to hundreds—or even thousands—of companies without having a ton of money to begin with.

So how are companies selected for each fund? There are two basic ways: active investing and passive investing. Active investing is when someone actively researches and selects which companies to invest in. This process is labor-intensive and more costly. Many actively managed funds are mutual funds, which we will discuss below. Passive investing is simply copying or indexing what someone else selects to be in a fund. It's where index funds come into play.

Index Funds

When you were in school and didn't feel like doing your assignment but it was due the following day, what did you do? You might have copied off your friend! (A smart friend, hopefully!) That's what index funds are. Portfolio managers copied the selection of stocks from an index to create the fund. It's called passive investing because there is minimal effort on the portfolio manager's part!

An index is a group of companies that collectively represents something, like a country's economy. S&P Dow Jones Indices, MSCI, and FTSE Russell are the three largest index providers in the world. They have experts and analysts doing all the research to put together groups (indices) of companies or products that collectively represent something.

For example, Standard & Poor put together the S&P 500, which represents the United States' economy and contains the 500 largest publicly listed companies in the country. A U.S. technology index would include all the technology giants such as Alphabet, Facebook, Amazon,

Apple, etc. Collectively, this group is a good representation of the U.S. technology sector.

The benefits of index funds are:

→ They are inexpensive to own because minimal effort is required by the portfolio manager.

→ You are diversified even when starting out with little money.

→ You don't need to spend time researching and tracking individual companies.

The drawback is that you don't get to choose which companies go into these funds. It means that although you own companies that are good, you will also own stock in poorly performing companies.

MONEY MATTERS: THE STOCK MARKET AVERAGE RETURN

When watching the news, any reference to "the markets" is a reference to an index. For example, when you hear people say, "The U.S. markets are down," they are generally referring to a decrease in the S&P 500 index value. Each country has its own stock index that represents the overall economy. Canada, for instance, uses the S&P/ TSX Composite index, which represents its stock markets.

The S&P 500 index has returned roughly 10% on average per year since its inception in 1927, when there were only ninety companies in the index. When you invest in an index fund that tracks a country's economy, you should be expecting roughly a stock market average return on your investments. It's a stock market average return because it includes so many companies—good or bad. The return is an average of excellent companies' performance and those that don't perform well.

Exchange-Traded Funds (ETFs)

One of the two ways you can invest in an index fund is through an exchange-traded fund (ETF). An exchange-traded fund is publicly listed on a stock exchange—like stocks—and available for anyone to buy or sell. The ETF creation process works a bit like this: ETF providers create funds by bundling up many stocks or bonds, then divide the fund into millions of tiny units, and list them on a stock exchange for people to buy and sell. Each ETF unit contains tiny fractional ownerships of hundreds or even thousands of companies or bonds.

ETFs can be funds that are actively managed or passively managed, though most are passively managed.

When you do your research on actively managed ETFs, you'll find that the fees, called the **management expense ratios (MERs)**, are much higher than passively managed ETFs. That's because the active component increases the cost of the fund—more people required to do research and select companies, for instance.

The benefits of ETFs are:

⇨ Anyone is free to buy and sell them because they are listed on a stock exchange.

⇨ There are no restrictions on the funds (unlike mutual funds, which we'll discuss later).

➔ They are diversified investments.

➔ You can start investing with little money.

The drawbacks of ETFs are:

➔ Like index funds, you have no control over the companies in the funds.

➔ They are subjected to the same market instability as stocks.

Here is what your ETF portfolio could look like:

Sample ETF Portfolio

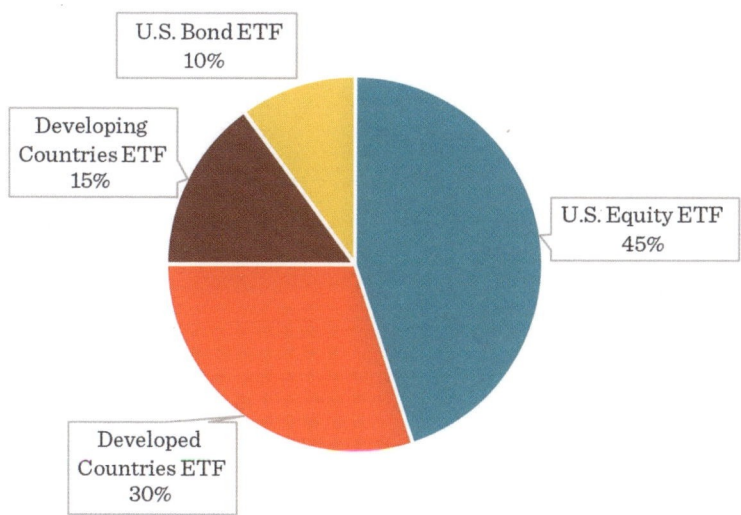

U.S. Bond ETF
10%

Developing
Countries ETF
15%

U.S. Equity ETF
45%

Developed
Countries ETF
30%

BUILDING YOUR DIVERSIFIED PORTFOLIO WITH ETFS

Do an online search for ETF providers. The largest providers are BlackRock and Vanguard, so you can start with those if you'd like.

Include equity ETFs. When building a portfolio, make sure you are geographically diverse, too. U.S. companies make up roughly 50% of global equities, so there's another 50% out there! Countries outside of the United States are categorized as developed (Germany, France, Singapore) or developing (Brazil, China, South Africa).

You can pick a global ETF that covers the entire world, or choose a few ETFs that each cover a specific region, like this:

➡ United States

➡ Developed countries outside the United States

➡ Emerging/developing countries

Add in some bond ETFs. Bond ETFs can be categorized into corporate, government, high-yield, short-term, long-term, etc. Investing in bond ETFs is the easiest way to access bonds and reduce the risk of your portfolio. Select one, two, or none, depending on your risk tolerance.

Fill out the table below for several equity and/or bond ETFs you're interested in to see how much you'll need to invest in each based on the unit price.

Name of Equity ETF	Ticker Symbol	Geographic Region Covered	Market Price per ETF Unit
Example: iShares Core S&P 500	IVV	United States	$435.95

Name of Bond ETF	Ticker Symbol	Types of Bonds (e.g., corporate, high-yield, government, short-term, long-term)	Market Price per ETF Unit
Example: iShares Core U.S. Aggregate Bond	AGG	U.S. investment-grade bonds	$109.86

Mutual Funds

Unlike ETFs, mutual funds are not exchange-listed. That means you must go through someone at a financial institution, like a bank or brokerage, to invest your money. Most mutual funds are actively managed, so they include fees paid to portfolio managers (operating costs). Mutual funds also include a sales component to compensate for the financial advice they provide to their clients. These fees are called **sales loads**, and can be charged on the front end, when you initially invest, or on the back end, when you sell your mutual funds. Mutual funds used to be very expensive (and some still are), but over the years these overall fees have been reduced with the introduction of low-cost ETFs.

Mutual funds may also include restrictions such as:

→ Minimum initial investments

→ Minimum ongoing investments (e.g., monthly invest-ments of $500)

→ Early-redemption charges (a fee for taking your money out before a specified period)

Because mutual funds are not exchange-listed, they are less liquid than ETFs. Each time an investor buys or sells their mutual fund, the transaction is executed at the end of the day (not immediately, as with stocks or ETFs). Also, when you invest in an actively managed fund, you're trusting the knowledge and judgment of the portfolio manager to select companies that will outperform the market average. You might want to consider investing in everything, earn an average return, and save on the fees instead.

SUCCESS STORY

One of my first clients, Sarah, held a portfolio of mutual funds that her bank set up for her. After reading my book and discovering how much cheaper ETFs were, she reached out and wanted me to take a look at her portfolio. In addition to paying high mutual fund fees, Sarah's portfolio was not appropriate for her. Like Jane from earlier, her money was invested in very low-risk options. Sarah was in her twenties, so she could definitely afford more risk. I helped revamp her portfolio and saved her more than $4,400 per year on average in fees alone!

Sarah's new investment strategy was very simple and the best option for her because it:

⬦ Consistently invested a portion of her paycheck every month into low-cost funds

⬦ Was diversified

⬦ Included the appropriate investments based on her risk tolerance

By the time she was thirty-six years old, Sarah's portfolio was worth almost $500,000!

CALCULATING FEES

Investment returns compound over time, but so can fees because MERs are deducted from the returns of the fund. For example, if a fund returns 8% in 2024, and the charged MER is 1%, your net return is 7%. If your portfolio is worth $1,000 in 2024, the cost is: $1,000 × 0.01 = $10.

It doesn't sound like a lot, does it? But imagine you started with $1,000 and then continued to invest $200 per month over a thirty-year period, and earned an average 8% return per year. By the end of thirty years, you would have paid $28,927 in fees, or $964 per year! This chart illustrates the accumulation of fees over a twenty- to thirty-year period.

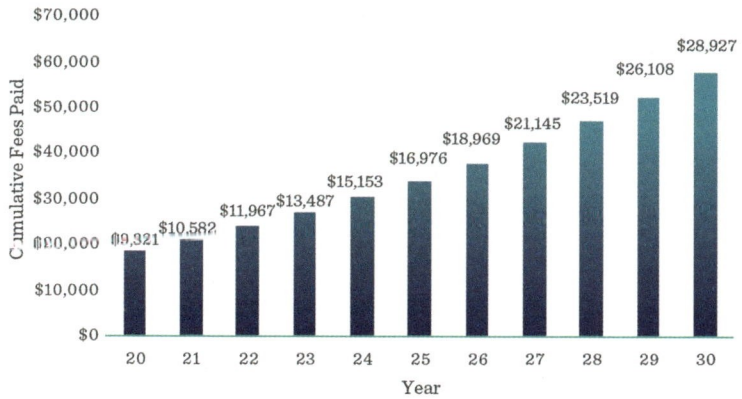

Fees Paid at a Rate of 1% from 20 to 30 Years

continued

CALCULATING FEES *continued*

Some passively managed funds have fees as low as 0.02%. Instead of charging $10 on a $1,000 investment per year, they charge $0.20. That's a huge difference! Write down the MER for the ETFs or mutual funds you want to invest in. Using the same compounding calcula- tor from chapter 2 (page 33), calculate how much these fees will cost you over a thirty-year period.

_____

_____

_____

_____

_____

_____

_____

_____

_____

_____

_____

_____

Capital Gains

When you sell your investments (and hopefully make a return), the government will take its cut in the form of a capital gains tax. The tax amount will depend on whether the investment was a short-term investment (held for one year or less) or a long-term investment. It will also take into account your taxable income for the year.

Short-term capital gains tax rates range from 10% to 37%, and long-term capital gains tax rates range from 0% to 20%. Let's say you earned $9,000 in 2024. You invested $800 in stocks and sold them for $1,200 four months later. Your short-term capital gain is: $1,200 – $800 = $400. The government will tax you on the $400 at a rate of 10%, which means you will owe: $400 × 0.10 = $40 in taxes. If you had waited as least a year to sell the stocks, you would be charged no capital gains tax on that amount.

Check Your Bottom Line

What you've learned in this chapter:

➔ How to diversify your investments

➔ What mutual funds, ETFs, and index funds are

➔ What stock market average return means

➔ The importance of watching out for the fees

➔ How capital gains taxes work

CHAPTER 7

Investing in Your Future

Nobody ever regrets saving too much money. But the opposite is true: I've met many people during my career—especially those nearing retirement—who regret not investing or saving money earlier in their lives. If you've come this far in this book, I can say confidently that you now know more than the average person about saving and investing.

Having savings and a nest egg gives you more choices in life. Look how Sam was able to move to Hawaii because of the safety net she built for herself! Although you may not be able to open a bank account or brokerage account on your own before you're eighteen years old, there are many things you can do now with the help of adults to get you set up for the future—like planning for college, career, and retirement.

We discussed checking and savings accounts in chapter 2, and brokerage accounts in chapter 5. In this section, you will discover the various accounts that are available for teens specifically, which accounts you might need, and how you can go about opening them.

There are two types of account you can open with your parent/guardian: a joint account or custodial account (which we briefly discussed in chapter 5).

Accounts for Teens

When you open a joint account, both you and your parent/guardian have equal ownership and control of it. There are teen accounts available (for those thirteen years and older). You may even be given a debit card. With it, you can make purchases with the cash in your account. This card also allows you to make cash withdrawals or deposit checks and cash into your account. I remember being super excited every time I made a deposit because my bank balance would increase!

Teen accounts are provided with more benefits than regular adult accounts, such as:

➔ Higher interest rates on savings

➔ No minimum balances

➔ No fees

Make it a habit to monitor your account on a weekly basis to keep track of your purchases and deposits. It's a great way to start establishing some financial independence and responsibility. You'll be able to access your account online or through a mobile app if the bank or credit union has one, and your parent/guardian will have access to the account for monitoring purposes. Use this account for everyday banking, such as purchases, withdrawals, and short- to medium-term savings.

UGMA AND UTMA ACCOUNTS

A custodial account is slightly different. It lists you (the minor) as the account owner, with a parent/guardian as the custodian (caretaker). This account would be managed by your parent/guardian and you would not have control or access to it until you reach eighteen years old (or twenty-one years old, depending on the state you live in).

Anything that is deposited into these accounts—whether it's from your parents/guardians, grandparents, or anyone else—belongs to you and cannot be taken back. That means it's permanent and nobody can legally use the money unless it's for your benefit. Consider your money protected!

There are two main types of custodial accounts: the Uniform Gifts to Minors Act (UGMA) account and the Uniform Transfers to Minors Act (UTMA) account. The main difference between UGMA and UTMA lies in what types of assets are allowed to be held in each.

A UGMA account allows you to hold financial assets like cash, stocks, and bonds. A UTMA account allows you to hold those same financial assets in addition to other assets, like real estate, collections, cars, or any asset your parent/guardian wants you to have ownership of.

There is one drawback for a UGMA/UTMA: Owning one will reduce the financial aid you receive when applying for college.

The tax benefits for these accounts are:

➔ Earnings up to $1,050 are tax-free.

➔ The next $1,050 is taxed to the minor (which will be lower than for the adult).

➔ Earnings over $2,100 are taxed to the parent/guardian.

Compared with a custodial Roth IRA as mentioned in chapter 5, UGMA/UTMA accounts do not have contribution limits or require earned income on your part. Use this account for longer-term savings and investments.

SETTING UP ACCOUNTS

In chapter 2, you made a list of your short-term and long-term goals. Recall that any short-term goals should be placed in a savings account, and any long-term goals involve investing your money. Now let's determine what accounts you need to open with your parent/guardian. Here is a summary of the types of accounts:

Accounts for Everyday Banking and Short-Term Savings:

➔ Joint savings/checking account

Custodial Brokerage Accounts for Investing and Long-Term Savings:

➔ UGMA/UTMA

  ➔ No contribution limits

  ➔ No income requirement

  ➔ Taxable on earnings

➔ Custodial Roth IRA (see chapter 5)

  ➔ Tax-free growth on earnings

  ➔ Earned income required

  ➔ Annual contribution limits

Start shopping online for these accounts by checking out various banks, credit unions, and bro-kerages. A good start is to see what is offered at your parent's/guardian's banks.

Planning for College

Everyone takes their own path after they graduate high school, whether it's taking a gap year or heading directly into post-secondary school. The most common types of post-secondary education are:

⇨ Four-year college or university to obtain an academic bachelor's degree

⇨ Two-year college (community college) to earn an Associate of Arts (AA) degree or an Applied Science (AAS) degree

⇨ Vocational college to learn the skills needed for a specific career (e.g., carpentry, plumbing)

I mentioned previously that the average cost of tuition in the United States is $35,331 per year, or $141,324 over four years. Your cost will vary based on which school you select. It's an overwhelming amount of money, but it's also an investment in your future that will pay off multiple times, plus provide you numerous career opportunities. You are certainly not expected to come up with the full amount by the time you start school, so we will discuss the various ways to help you plan and pay for your education.

529 COLLEGE SAVINGS PLAN

One of the most common ways adults save for their kids' education is through a 529 college savings plan, which is a tax-advantaged account a parent/guardian starts on their child's behalf. They contribute and invest, and the money grows tax-free. Your parent or guardian must open this account/plan and name you as the beneficiary.

When you start college, you can withdraw money from this account tax-free and apply it to qualified higher education expenses, such as tuition, room and board, books, computers, and software (if required). You may even use the money for some non-U.S. schools. This plan offers flexibility because you're not committed to a specific college or university and you can use the money for costs outside of tuition.

FINANCIAL AID

Given how much colleges/universities cost, it's no surprise that many people are unable to save enough for the entire cost. That's where financial aid comes in handy. Financial aid is a combination of grants, loans, scholarships, and work-study programs.

> **Grants:** Grant money is given to those that need financial help. They don't have to be repaid (unless you breach a condition, like drop out of a specific program), and you may receive this from the federal government, state government, your college/university, or other organizations.

> **Work-Study Program:** This is a federal work program that allows students to work at participating schools to earn money part-time. The money they earn helps pay for school.

Student Loans: The government, banks, and other organizations lend money to students. That money must be repaid, with interest.

Federal Student Aid is part of the U.S. Department of Education. It helps students and families pay for post-secondary education. You can apply for financial aid using FAFSA® (Free Application for Federal Student Aid) on their website. When you receive a financial aid package, it may include a combination of grants, loans, and/or work-study programs. Financial aid is calculated based on your financial need. It takes into account what your family contributes (Expected Family Contribution/ EFC). Their tax returns, statement of assets, and income will be factored in.

If you've been accepted to multiple schools, each school may provide you with different grants or school aid, so be sure to compare what you receive from each school so you can assess what you can afford. There are federal deadlines for each academic year, so be sure to stay on top of it!

SCHOLARSHIPS

Imagine doing what you love and what you're good at while having your education paid for. It's possible! For example, you may be a competitive swimmer who is accepted to a school on a partial or full scholarship to swim on the school team while pursing your education. Scholarships are given to students based on academic excellence or talent in a specific subject, like the arts and athletics. They do not need to be repaid, though they are dependent on continued performance in whatever the scholarship is for, like sports.

Many of my friends who have been awarded scholarships, especially for athletics and arts, had much of their family supporting them. Weekend tournaments out of state, weekly practices, and competitions all require a level of financial and time commitment from your household. It costs money to attend events and receive coaching. Of course, you also must invest time improving your talents.

Schools want to recruit the best people for their teams, so getting a scholarship will be competitive and labor-intensive on your end. You want to stand out and catch their attention! If you're interested in an academic scholarship, like math, there are contests that you can participate in. They will certainly help your résumé and application if you do well!

If you're interested in an athletic scholarship, check out the College Scholarships USA website to learn about the process. Scholarships.com is another great resource that can help you find scholarships of any kind. If you're interested in attending a specific school, check out their website to see what their requirements, timeline, and process are for obtaining a scholarship.

STUDENT LOANS

Student loans are often a big portion of a student's financial aid package. They allow many students to pursue post-secondary education when they might not otherwise have been able to. There are two types of federal loans: direct subsidized loans and direct unsubsidized loans. Direct subsidized loans are available to students who need financial aid. The government pays the loan's interest throughout school and for the first six months after graduation. Direct unsubsidized loans are available to any student, even if they don't have a financial need. For this type of loan, the student is responsible for all of the interest payments until the loan is paid.

Although it may be tempting to take out a big loan upfront, skip a part-time job while in school, and pay for the entire loan once you graduate, it might not be the best thing to do for your future self. One of the things I failed to plan for was my post-secondary education. I assumed—between working in an internship program between semesters, and applying for student loans—that I would be able to cover all my expenses. For the most part, I did, but I messed up because I was a Susie Spender. I stopped being eligible for student loans because of how much I earned in my internships. I saved enough money for my tuition but not enough for my other expenses, so I had to use my credit cards to make up the difference.

The less student debt you graduate with, the better—even if it means working during the summer, taking part-time jobs, and spending the time to apply for grants.

MONEY MATTERS:
YOUR MILLION-DOLLAR PORTFOLIO

The sooner you start investing for your retirement, the less money you'll need to invest. Let's assume an annual return rate of 8%. If you give yourself forty-eight years to build your $1 million invest-ment portfolio, you only need to invest $50 per month—and increase the monthly payments by $10 each year. You will max out at investing $520 per month in year forty-eight!

If you give yourself twenty-nine years to invest for retirement, you'll need to invest $750 per month while increasing the monthly payments by $10 each year to hit $1 million. You will max out at $1,020 per month in your twenty-eighth year.

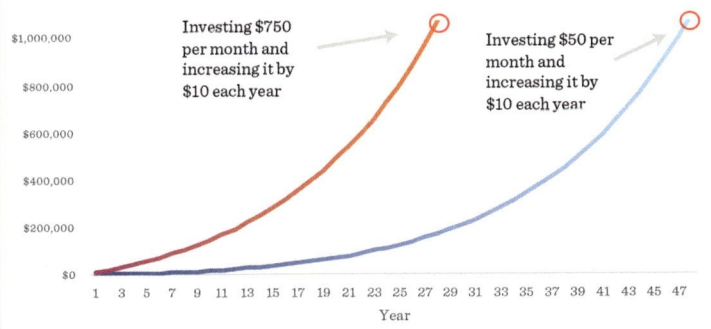

Savings Growth with an 8% Annual Return

Planning for Your Career

It is never too early to think about your future career prospects and goals!

I have friends who switched programs in school numerous times. They pursued degrees just for the sake of getting an education without much thought about their purpose and intention. Can you guess what happened? Many graduated with a boatload of debt while working the same part-time job they had during their post-secondary education.

There is no right way to pursue your life. Everyone has their own path and decides what's best for themselves. However, part of making smart financial decisions is planning for goals—including your education or anything that has a price tag.

The earlier you start exploring the career paths and opportunities that are out there, the more time you will give yourself to plan and make good decisions about your post-secondary education, which is a giant investment.

So how do you start planning for a career? Here are some things to think about.

⇨ **What you're interested in:** Your passions are a good place to start. When I was a teen, I was very into computers. I built a website that generated a ton of traffic and asked my family to call me "MicroMich" because I wanted to be the next Bill Gates. I got accepted into a computer science program, but ultimately chose a math and business program instead. I ended up hating computer programming after failing a computer science course my first year of college.

During high school, I developed a very keen interest in business . . . and I also happened to be good at math. After exploring several potential career paths through my internships and conversations with adults, I eventually figured out finance was the path I wanted to take. Speaking to adults from various industries inspired me most, so if you have an area of interest, start asking your friends and family about who they can connect you with.

→ **Where to study:** So you have an idea of the type of career you want to pursue. Great! The next thing you should do is research the schools that specialize in the education for that career or are well-known for attracting employers that hire graduates from those programs.

You'll probably have a top school in mind with a few backups. Check their entry requirements and start preparing to meet those requirements. It may mean improving your GPA or participating in more extracurricular activities.

Make sure you also research companies you are interested in working for. Check to see if they hire students during the summer months, or if they hire fresh grads from specific schools. For example, many prestigious Wall Street banks like Goldman Sachs or Morgan Stanley tend to hire undergrads from Ivy League schools like Wharton School or Harvard. If you're interested in social media, a digital marketing program may be right for you. Search for schools that offer that.

→ **How much schooling is required?** Does your career require education beyond an undergraduate degree? If so, what does that look like? For example, lawyers and doctors require many more years of study after post-secondary—which means more money for tuition and a delay in starting work.

If you're interested in pursuing a master's or doctorate degree, you are going to require more schooling and more loans, and have less money-earning potential in the short term. There are many doctors in their forties who are still paying off their student loans. In the end, with their high salaries, there is no doubt they will eventually finish paying them off—but not everyone who pursues a master's or doctorate degree earns a high salary.

So with that said . . .

➔ **Will it pay off?** Keep in mind how much you expect to make in your career versus the cost to pursue it. It never really made sense to me that some people spend over $250,000 on a degree, only to make $50,000 per year before taxes because their chosen industry limits people's salaries.

This is how people get stuck paying their student loans for years!

Certain industries will limit a person's pay, no matter how much they succeed. On the flip side, other industries are desperate for workers, so they are willing to pay a lot of money to attract people with a specific skill or qualification.

Consider where your chosen industry will be headed in the next several decades. Will its jobs be obsolete? Will technology take over and automate everything? Some research is required on your end. Imagine investing more than $100,000 in an education, years of studies, and learning a skill that will no longer be required because it was replaced by a robot!

➔ **Where to live?** I grew up in the biggest city in Canada—Toronto. It is *the* place to live for any Canadian pursuing a job in finance because the head offices of the big banks are in the city. Likewise, in the United States, many aspiring financiers congregate to New York City in hopes of landing a prestigious job on Wall Street. If you're an aspiring tech guru, Silicon Valley in California is the place to be.

If you're from a small town with limited opportunities, you'll probably have to relocate unless you can work remotely. Consider where you might have to move once you discover where your job opportunities are located. Many of my friends from abroad moved to Canada for better job opportunities and a chance to create a better life than they would have had if they stayed home.

Planning for Your Retirement

Imagine what your life would be like if you didn't have to go to school, didn't have to work, and could do whatever you wanted every single day. It's how most people define retirement. Typically, people aren't able to retire until they're in their sixties.

You might be wondering, *Why am I even thinking about something that is decades away?* Remember how I mentioned I was laid off from my job when I was thirty-one years old, but had my $100,000 investment portfolio, so I did whatever I wanted without worrying about money? That's why.

Saving and investing for your future is not just about retiring in your sixties. Your money and investments will come in handy if you stop working at any point in your life! If you stash away enough money, you may even be able to retire well before you're in your sixties! So what are the best ways to plan for retirement? Read on to find out!

IRA

Taxes will be your biggest bills in life, so it's worth taking the time to see how you can reduce this expense! When you invest in an IRA (individual retirement account), you are getting several benefits:

→ A reduced tax bill for the year you contribute to the account

→ Tax-free growth on all investment earnings—including interest, dividends, and capital gains

An IRA is a tax-deferred account. That means you don't pay taxes on your investment earnings or employment income you invest in it. You pay taxes when you withdraw money during your retirement (when you will hopefully be in a lower tax bracket). Money contributed to this account reduces your current tax bill, so we call this pre-tax money. On the other hand, a Roth IRA is an after-tax account because you fund it with income you've already paid taxes on. All investment earnings grow tax-free and when you withdraw from the account you won't pay any taxes at all.

401(K)

When you work full-time at a company, your employer may offer you benefits such as a 401(k) plan. 401(k)s are employer-sponsored plans that allow you to save and invest in your retirement with the help of your employer.

Like an IRA, a 401(k) is a pre-tax account and investment earnings grow tax-free.

For example, if your employer offers a 401(k) plan where you contribute a percentage of your salary and they match it 100%, your retirement investment is doubled. Say you earn $57,000 per year and you contribute 6% of your salary to the 401(k). Then your employer matches 100% of it. You're putting away this much from your own paycheck:

6% × $57,000 = $3,420

When your employer matches 100% of what you contribute, you're actually stashing away:

$3,420 × 2 = $6,840 in your retirement account!

It's free money, so make sure you take advantage of these benefits offered as part of your overall compensation at your job!

PENSIONS

A pension plan is also an employer-sponsored plan. The employer makes contributions to your retirement fund (you may also contribute) *and* manages the money on your behalf. When you retire, they pay you a specific monthly income for life; therefore, they bear the investment risk. It differs from the 401(k), Roth IRA, and IRA, where you are responsible for putting money into your retirement funds, bearing the investment risk, and making sure your money lasts until you die!

It doesn't matter how bad the stock markets are doing; you are promised your payments (unless the company goes bankrupt). Having a guaranteed income during retirement is incredible. Imagine receiving a salary forever without working! Make sure you know roughly how much pension income you'll receive, because it may not be enough to fund all your expenses during retirement.

SOCIAL SECURITY

Social security is another form of pension that is sponsored by the government. As an American taxpayer, you are entitled to retirement benefits. What you receive depends on when you retire and how much you earned during your working years. You pay a social security tax during your working years and the government manages that money on your behalf. In turn, you will receive continuous payments until you die.

The more you earn, and the later you wait to start collecting social security, the higher your monthly benefit payment will be. To give you an idea of what these payments may look like, the maximum benefit a person could receive in 2024 if they retired at sixty-six years old (full retirement age) is $4,873 per month, or $58,476 a year. These payments go up every year to keep up with inflation.

When planning for retirement, it's critical to plan out where your sources of income will come from to make sure you don't run out of money!

I went to a university that was known for placing students in internships between academic semesters. I went to school for four months, then worked for four months—on and off for almost five years. The sacrifice I made was not playing varsity soccer. Although I have a bit of regret, it was worth it in the end. I was never going to be a professional soccer player anyway! Instead, I graduated with two years of work experience and was more employable than my peers who didn't do internships.

Many of my friends who did internships like I did were able to:

◇ Earn money that helped pay for school

◇ Gain valuable work experience

◇ Get a head start in their careers

All these things led to us becoming financially well off earlier than our peers. We were more employable, paid off debt sooner, started saving sooner, and bought real estate first. If you can get internships during the summer, I highly recommend it!

CAREER PLANNING

Now's the time to start brainstorming your potential career paths. Follow these steps.

1. Write down your interests and what you're passionate about.

2. Write down what your skills are and things you want to improve.

3. Research careers and industries that involve the skills and interests you wrote down.

4. Make a list of people you may know (e.g., family and friends) who might be able to connect you with professionals who are working in the industries or careers you listed.

5. Research post-secondary schools that offer programs that will put you on a strong path to that career.

6. Start working on building the skills that will help you with your career. For example, if you want to become a computer developer, start learning how to code. Do a search online for free courses or talk to teachers at your school about how to get resources you need. If it turns out you hate coding, then training to be a developer is not for you!

Aim High

Congratulations! You are now financially literate and have gained an important life skill—how to make and manage a life resource: *money*. What are your goals? Maybe it's planning a worldwide trip, retiring at thirty-five years old, sending your children to school, or simply making the world a better place. You now have the tools and knowledge to start planning and executing. Almost everything involves money, so the more you have (and save!), the more options you give yourself, making life much less stressful.

I mentioned it earlier and I'll say it again: You gain the most advantage simply by being young and starting your investing journey early. You will be faced with choices like buying the latest cell phone now or investing the money for future use. They will be difficult decisions because we all like to live in the moment, but more times than not, your future self will thank you for the choice you made in that moment.

If there are three pieces of advice I could give to my teenage self, they would be: stay out of debt, invest as early as possible, and never cap your earnings potential. There is so much wealth out there, and you just learned several ways to build it—by saving, investing, or starting a business. Aim high, and when you feel you have a good goal, aim even higher! You are only as big as the dream you dare to live.

Check Your Bottom Line

What you've learned in this chapter:

⇨ Different types of accounts you can open

⇨ How to plan for your education and how to pay for it

⇨ How to plan for your career

⇨ What retirement is and when to start investing for it (today!)

GLOSSARY

annual percentage yield (APY): the real rate of return earned on an investment, including compound interest

asset: something valuable you own—like a house, stocks, or cash—that can be used for financial benefit

bear market: the state of the stock market when stock prices decline at least 20% over a prolonged period

blockchain: a digital record or database of transactions that are stored and dispensed online in a decentralized manner (a digital list of transactions that can be seen by everybody and edited by nobody, but anyone can add to the list if they follow the rules)

bond: a low-risk loan an investor can make to a company in return for interest on that loan

brokerage: an institution that connects buyers and sellers to make things like stock and bond transactions easy

budget: a system that helps you organize your expenses relative to your income

bull market: the state of the stock market when stock prices rise at least 20% over a prolonged period

capital: things of value, like money, that can be used to make more money

capital gain: the profit you make when you sell an asset

certificate of age: an official document, certifying age, that permits the employment of a minor

compound interest: the accumulated interest earned from your savings, plus the interest on the interest you earned

coupon: the annual interest rate paid on a bond

credit: money loaned that needs to paid back later (often with interest)

credit union: a nonprofit financial institution that is owned by its members and offers things like loans, bank accounts, and credit cards

currency: the money issued by a country

debit card: a card used for purchases that takes money directly from your bank account

debt: money owed to one party by another

default risk: the possibility that a borrower does not repay their debt or interest to the lender

equity: the value of owned assets like stocks or real estate

fair market value: the price someone would pay for an asset determined by the buyers and sellers in an open market

fiat currency: government-issued currency in the form of paper money or coins that are not backed by any physical gold or silver

financial statements: written documents that show the status of a company's financial position and profit and loss

fixed expense: expenses that are predictable in cost and recurrence

fund: a pool of money that is invested in hundreds or thousands of companies in the form of stock, bonds, or both

income statement: a financial statement that shows a company's profit or loss

index: companies grouped into categories that collectively represent something (e.g., S&P 500 index)

indirect costs: the costs of running a business that are not included in the direct manufacturing or development of a product or service (such as marketing)

inflation: the loss of the value of money over time leading to increased prices

interest: a fee charged for borrowing money

Internal Revenue Service (IRS): the U.S. federal agency responsible for tax collection

invest: spending money to make money work for you

line of credit: a type of loan that allows you to borrow money up to a pre-set limit

management expense ratio (MER): the total fee for the management of a fund expressed as a percentage of the average total assets managed for the year

mortgage: a loan used to purchase a property, like a home

net income: a company's profit after all expenses and taxes are deducted from revenue

non-fungible token (NFT): a digital asset (music, images, or videos) that can be bought and sold over blockchains

passive income: earnings from a source that doesn't require effort, like a dividend stock or rental property

personal loan: money borrowed with an agreement to repay the amount over a fixed period, including interest

portfolio: a collection of investments that could include things like stocks, bonds, rental properties, and cash

principal: the money used as an original investment

real gross domestic product (real GDP): the value of the goods and services produced by an economy over a specific period, adjusted for inflation

return: the money you make or lose on an investment over time

sales loads: the money paid to a financial adviser or broker for the sale of a mutual fund

security: an asset that can be bought, sold, or traded

shareholder: a person or institution that owns at least one share of a company's stock

stock: a fractional share of ownership in a company

stock market: where stocks are bought and sold

variable expense: expenses that vary monthly, weekly, or daily

venture capitalist: an investor that gives money to a private company with high growth prospects in exchange for a percentage of the company's ownership

work permit: an official document that allows a minor to be employed

RESOURCES

Additional Books on Investing

One Up on Wall Street by Peter Lynch
A beginner's book about picking individual stocks

The Sassy Investor by Michelle Hung
A step-by-step guide on how to invest in the stock markets

The Warren Buffett Way by Robert G. Hagstrom
Deep insights and investment strategies from one of the world's greatest investors

Online Resources

Dividend Growth Investor: a blog focused on dividend growth stocks
dividendgrowthinvestor.com

Erika Kullberg: attorney and personal finance expert dedicated to making legal advice accessible for entrepreneurs and business owners
erikakullberg.com

Investing with Rose: a YouTube channel dedicated to money and investing

youtube.com/c/InvestingWithRose

Morningstar: an economic news and company research site

morningstar.com

TeenVestor: a site dedicated to teen investing

teenvestor.com

Wall Street Survivor: a site where you can build a practice stock portfolio and challenge your friends to a contest

wallstreetsurvivor.com

INDEX

Acknowledgments

I am so grateful to my colleagues, friends, and mentors who I have learned so much from in the corporate and personal finance space.

To my students and audience—thank you for your time and energy, and for giving me a space to grow as a teacher, mentor, and influencer.

To my incredible family and friends who have kept me on track writing this book and celebrated with me: Sean, Mary, Daniella, Sarina, Patrick, Jamie, Flor, Ellie, Christian, Martyna, Veronique, Anton, Allistair, Rob, Will, Oliver, and Heather.

Finally, a very special thank you to my mom, dad, and sister, Cheryl. Your unconditional love and support know no bounds.

About the Author

Michelle Hung, CFA, is an author and the founder of *The Sassy Investor*, a platform for empowering women to take control of their finances and to build a lifetime of wealth. Michelle graduated from the University of Waterloo with a bachelor's degree in mathematics, specializing in finance. In 2014, she achieved the Chartered Financial Analyst (CFA) designation. For more information on Michelle, visit thesassyinvestor.ca or email her at info@thesassyinvestor.ca.